GOD IS GOOD,
EVEN WHEN LIFE IS HARD

*A story of experiencing
God's goodness in the
midst of hardships*

Katie Poindexter *with* Angela Wold

WESTBOW
PRESS®
A DIVISION OF THOMAS NELSON
& ZONDERVAN

WestBow Press books may be ordered through booksellers or by contacting:

WestBow Press
A Division of Thomas Nelson & Zondervan
1663 Liberty Drive
Bloomington, IN 47403
www.westbowpress.com
1 (866) 928-1240

Because of the dynamic nature of the Internet, any web addresses or links contained in this book may have changed since publication and may no longer be valid. The views expressed in this work are solely those of the author and do not necessarily reflect the views of the publisher, and the publisher hereby disclaims any responsibility for them.

Any people depicted in stock imagery provided by Getty Images are models, and such images are being used for illustrative purposes only. Certain stock imagery © Getty Images.

Scripture quotations are from the ESV® Bible (The Holy Bible, English Standard Version®), copyright © 2001 by Crossway, a publishing ministry of Good News Publishers. Used by permission. All rights reserved.

Scripture quotations marked (NLT) are taken from the Holy Bible, New Living Translation, copyright © 1996, 2004, 2007 by Tyndale House Foundation. Used by permission of Tyndale House Publishers, Inc., Carol Stream, Illinois 60188. All rights reserved.

THE HOLY BIBLE, NEW INTERNATIONAL VERSION®, NIV® Copyright © 1973, 1978, 1984, 2011 by Biblica, Inc.® Used by permission. All rights reserved worldwide.

ISBN: 978-1-9736-7190-9 (sc)
ISBN: 978-1-9736-7192-3 (hc)
ISBN: 978-1-9736-7191-6 (e)

Library of Congress Control Number: 2019911600

Print information available on the last page.

WestBow Press rev. date: 8/29/2019

To Stephen Reynolds:
You never stopped loving me, and you never
stopped encouraging me to seek after Christ.
You impacted many people through your love for Christ.
Thank you for loving me so well!

To the Reynolds family, my family, and friends:
Thank you to every one of you that has
encouraged me in my season of loss.
I cherish you! You all are a blessing, and I thank God for you!

ACKNOWLEDGEMENTS

I want to thank God for His unconditional love, comfort, and peace that He has given me. You never left my side. God you are ever so faithful. I am so blessed to be Your child.

Angela, dear Angela, I want to thank you for all your work on this manuscript! You have been a constant blessing as you edited this book. Thank you for all your hard work! You helped me fill in the gaps and communicate more clearly than I was able to do on my own. I am forever grateful for your willingness to help me with the project. I am so glad God allowed us to work together. Thank you for everything you have done!

Lizzie Lindberg, I'm so thankful for your artist talents in designing the cover for this book. Thank you for allowing God to use you in the process.

Mrs. Reynolds and Mr. Reynolds, you both have been an encouragement to me as I wrote this book. If it wasn't for your suggestion to tell my story, I may never have thought to write this book. You both have blessed me in indescribable ways. Thank you for your continued love, support, and friendship. I will always view you as my family. You have blessed me tremendously, and I thank God for you!

Troy and Elise Frasier, Stephen and Grace Buller, Carolyn and Daniel Frey, and Jill Ann and Jered Jerome, you four couples have been an encouragement to me in so many different ways! Thank you for allowing God to use you. Thank you all for blessing me with friendship, encouragement, love, and time. Troy, Buller, Carolyn and Jill, I am forever grateful that you were willing to grieve Stephen with me, talk about loss with me, and have continued to be true brothers and sisters in Christ! I thank God for you!

Mom and Dad, thank you for leading me by example in your faith. Without your encouragement to seek God and follow Him, I don't know where I'd be. Thank you for teaching me about God's love, Jesus' sacrifice, and the Holy Spirit's presence. Thank you for encouraging me to try new things, to attend a Bible college, and to meet new people. I'm not sure what kind of person I would be without you both. Thank you for loving me and being there for me whenever I need it. You were constantly there for me during these years of hardships. Thank you for everything! I love you!

My brother Jonathan, you have always been loving and protective of me. I am thankful that you have been and still are supportive in my life. Thank you for being there for me in my loss. Thank you for allowing God to use you to encourage me. You are a blessing, Jonathan, and I'm so thankful for your encouragement in this book process!

All my Calvary brothers and sisters, each one of you has impacted my life and has been an encouragement in my healing process. Thank you for allowing God to use you to help lessen my brokenness by all your hugs, prayers, and encouragement. You all are a blessing!

I especially want to thank my Calvary professors Mrs. M. and Mr. Smith. You taught Stephen and me about God and how to think through what we believe. You taught Stephen and me how to work through emotions and healing from past hurts. Our faith became stronger through your teaching and mentoring. Stephen is no longer here, but I know he would wish to tell you, "Thank you." Thank you for allowing God to use you in our lives and in so many other Calvary students' lives. Thank you also for your encouragement as I wrote this book. You have blessed me so much!

Everyone else, my family, the Reynolds family, old friends,

and new friends, you have encouraged me to seek God. You have prayed for me, hugged me, laughed with me, cried with me, and loved me. I am so blessed by God to have a big support group such as you. Thank you for all the ways you have helped me through my brokenness, grief, loss, joy, and healing. God is to be praised for blessing me with all of you!

CONTENTS

PART 2: THINGS GOD TAUGHT ME THROUGH LOSS

PART 3: TYING IT ALL TOGETHER

INTRODUCTION

"God is good all the time, and all the time God is good."

The phrase, "God is good," is used all around the world. To some it gives hope, but to others, it is just a flippant phrase. I have come to see that simply saying, "God is good," and truly believing it and letting it affect my life are two different things. For me, the journey of going from simply knowing that God is good to really, truly believing it began seven years ago.

Sometimes the phrase, "God is good," gets tossed around and loses its significance. But when people hear the story of someone who has lived through sorrow and hardship and still says, "God is good," the phrase holds more weight. God has given me the ability to say this phrase with the weight of my story attached to it. I have experienced heart-wrenching loss and harsh physical suffering. To this day, I deal with physical pain on a daily basis. Yet my faith in God has not been shaken. My foundation in Christ remains strong. God is my Rock, and without Him I am nothing. If I would have walked through the heart-rending experiences recorded in this book without God, I would have become a poor, lost soul. Instead, I walked with my good God through all these hardships. He is my Father. I am His daughter, and He never left my side. On the days I truly knew God was good, I would smile and tell people about my good and gracious God. On the days when I was in so much pain that I could only see a glimpse of God's goodness, I would tearfully look people in the eye and tell them, "Life is very hard, and God is still good." Some days I struggled to truly believe that God really is good. On those hard days, I would repeat the phrase, "God is good," over and over again to remind myself that it was still true, even if I couldn't feel it at the moment.

I never really understood the comfort and power available to me in the Bible until the events of this book. Proverbs 16:3 says, "Commit your work to the Lord, and your plans will be established." Through these recorded events in my life, God has guided me, broken me, humbled me, and matured me. All I ask is that you read my story with an open mind. It is my hope that you begin to learn, without a shadow of a doubt, that God takes care of those who put their hope in Him. I have learned I cannot live my life by wanting to do things my way. Life is not about me. It is not about my plans, or what I want to do. Just like the Proverb says, if I commit my way to God, my plans will be established. However, they won't be my plans. They will be God's plans for my life because I have committed my plans to His care.

You will notice I placed Bible verses at the beginning of every chapter. I also have Bible verses scattered throughout the book. I realize that's a lot of Scripture. But this is my story, and my faith in God and the Bible is a huge part of my story. My faith is what got me through the difficulties and hardships. It's part of who I am as a person. If I were to take away my faith, I would no longer be the person I truly am. Many of these chosen verses were the ones that encouraged and helped me during the trials I faced. My hope is that they will encourage you as well. Most of the verses are from the English Standard Version (ESV) Bible translation. There are some from the New International Version (NIV) translation, and I have made those notations.

So with a humble heart, I begin a hard story of many tears yet much laughter. I am about to tell you my story and the story of Stephen Reynolds. It might not be the story you expect. It certainly wasn't what I expected. This is the journey that taught me to say, without hesitation, "God is good!"

We all have a story to tell, and this is mine. A story of God's goodness.

PART 1

OUR STORY AND THE MEMORIES THAT COME WITH IT

CHAPTER 1

Psalm 27: 13
*I believe that I shall look upon the goodness
of the Lord in the land of the living!*

MEETING STEPHEN REYNOLDS

It was August 2011. Summertime had just begun to fade, and all of us returning college students were driving on the roads that led back to our dormitories. The reunion of college friends after the summer was always exciting, and stories were shared of summer activities. As an upper classman, I (Katie) headed back to the dorms to see my friends. I was attending Calvary Bible College in Kansas City, Missouri. When I arrived, many freshman and transfer students had already moved into the dorms. I politely said, "Hello," to the freshman students as I looked for my friends so we could swap stories. We had a good time reuniting with laughter, hugs, and stories of the summer.

One of the exciting parts of the first week of school was meeting many new people. Working in the school cafeteria gave me an excellent opportunity to meet and develop relationships with the new students. One of the new students was Stephen Reynolds, a transfer student from Allen Community College in Lola, Kansas. The first time I met Stephen was in the school cafeteria during the first week of school. He was sitting and talking with his new-found friend Jon at one of the tables. Part of my cafeteria job was to walk around after everyone had left and clean all the tables. As I neared the end of my job, Stephen and Jon were at the last table to clean. They were both quite chatty with lively, fun personalities. I stood and talked with them for a few minutes to get to know them a little better.

I remember Jon introduced himself first. We both found it odd and exciting that his name was Jon, and he had a sister named Katie. I have a brother named Jonathan and my name, well obviously, is Katie! We knew it would always be easy to remember each other's names. Stephen was funny (always smiling and trying to make a joke) but quiet (never going out of his way to talk). He shook my hand and told me to always be real with him. I remember looking him straight in the eye, smiling, and telling him that I'd always be real with him. To this day I have kept my promise. I was always real with him. "Being real" is being honest about who you are and what you are going through in life. It also means speaking the truth with genuine love and honesty. The Lord knew that this first meeting of Stephen and Katie was to be the start of something great for His glory and for His Kingdom.

THE WOLFPACK

After a few weeks of school had gone by, something fun and exciting began to happen among many of the new transfer and freshman guys on campus. They became a close-knit group that eventually included some girls as well. We called the group "the Wolfpack." We gathered together for fun and laughter. But we truly cherished the times we got together to worship God, share our testimonies, and help keep each other strong in our Christian faith. I showed the Wolfpack one of my favorite places in Kansas City, a place my friends and I nicknamed "The River." It is a beautiful river surrounded by trees, walking trails, and lovely nature nooks. It became a tradition for the Wolfpack to go to The

River and share our testimonies around a campfire whenever the weather permitted. Some of the leaders of the Wolfpack decided the name Wolfpack needed to mean something other than the guys leaning their heads back and howling very loudly in the school cafeteria. They wanted this group to mean something more.

Stephen Reynolds, who was the main leader of the group, and a few other wolfpack guys created an acronym for the Wolfpack. Wolfpack came to mean Worship, Obedience, Leadership, Fellowship, Praise, Accountability, Christ-Likeness and Knowledge. Now that our name Wolfpack stood for something Christ-honoring, we became a group purposefully helping each other stay true to our faith. In one aspect, it was like a Bible Study group. But in other ways, it was so much more than that. The Wolfpack would have praise and worship services, prayer groups, community service outings, and so much more. It was a group of friends getting together for fun, but we also desired to make a point of glorifying God and honoring Him in everything we did. It was always a loudly joyful time of praising God together.

Stephen became the leader of all the guys. He would check up on them once a week, laugh about life with them, sit and listen to them during the hard times, and pray with them. God gave Stephen the biggest heart to love others that I've ever seen. The Holy Spirit gave Stephen the ability to love and challenge those young men as Stephen simply sought to be a good friend to all the guys in the Wolfpack. Yet as fun as Stephen could be with them, he kept them accountable to their faith in their lives. He also asked them to keep him accountable in the areas of life that were a struggle for him.

Desiring accountability and spiritual growth, I became the leader of the girls as more girls joined the Wolfpack. I would check up on the girls during the week and pray with them. Sometimes we would all get together and pray. There is nothing more awesome then seeing people get together to pray. Stephen and I would also check in with each other throughout the week to see how things were going and to make sure we were on the same page. We became close friends during this time and the Wolfpack continued to grow. The awesome thing was we were all being held accountable and growing in our faith! It was a marvelous kind of growth! Many of us who were part of the Wolfpack that first year will tell you to this day how it challenged us to grow in our faith. We have many memories of what God did during that time. That year was a season of growth. We simply wanted to grow in our faith, and we certainly did. We were inspired by each other's faith to continue to grow in our relationship with God.

STEPHEN'S DREAM FOR FUTURE KIDS

In September 2011, a few months after I met Stephen, I was sitting at a lunch table with a group of friends one day. Stephen was with us. We were all laughing, having a good time, and talking about our futures. Stephen loudly proclaimed that he was going to have 16 children. He smiled broadly, sat back in his chair, and started to recite their names. "Stephen Jr. will be number one, Stephanie if it's a girl. Stephon for the second boy...," he kept going as he and the other guys started laughing about his dream. I was shocked that he wanted 16 kids and asked, "Are you going to adopt or have all 16?" With a wide grin, Stephen answered, "Me and my wife gonna have 'em' all!" Not realizing I was thinking out loud, I responded, "Your poor wife!"

Little did I know that Stephen and I would be dating eight months later!

The idea of having a big family was something on which we agreed during our dating relationship. I wanted 10 kids, but Stephen was always set on having 16 kids. Whenever we talked about marriage, Stephen would always want to jump ahead and start naming our kids and talking about their futures. To this day, I smile at how much he wanted to have a family and teach his children the Word of God. He was passionate about it. We were both passionate about it. We agreed that if God would bless us with children, we wanted to love them and teach them God's love.

CHAPTER 2

Proverbs 3:3-6
Let not steadfast love and faithfulness forsake you; bind
them around your neck; write them on the tablet of your
heart. So you will find favor and good success in the sight
of God and man. Trust in the lord with all your heart, and
do not lean on your own understanding. In all your ways
acknowledge him, and he will make straight your paths.

THE BEGINNING OF THE ROMANCE

Prince Charming fought hard and gallantly to win the girl of his
dreams. The Princess, however, was totally and utterly clueless to
any romantic feelings Prince Charming had for her. It was up to
Prince Charming to show the Princess how much he loved her.

I was completely clueless of Stephen's true feelings toward me.
Let me begin the story of Prince Charming and his Princess.

DEER HUNTING ON MY FARM

In November 2011, Stephen and four other Calvary students
joined me for deer hunting at my farm in South Dakota. I love to
go deer hunting! It was quite the experience for my friends to visit
South Dakota during deer hunting season. We drove through a
blizzard to get to my house. None of them had ever experienced

a South Dakota blizzard! Since we arrived at 1:00 in the morning on Saturday, we slept late into the morning and went hunting in the afternoon. We went out to join the other hunters wearing our snow boots, coveralls, hats, mittens, and orange vests. The other hunters explained the ways of hunting to my friends. Since my five friends did not have guns, I decided not to carry a gun. I was a spotter instead. We all walked and waited for deer. Although I can't remember if the hunters got any deer, I do remember enjoying being out in God's beautiful nature. We had a fun weekend, and my parents enjoyed getting to know my friends. On Sunday, we left to return to school for Monday classes. Hence, Stephen had the opportunity to meet my parents. At the time, I didn't invite him to my house to purposefully meet my parents. I just enjoyed bringing my friends home to my farm.

A BOTTLE OF WATER

I remember the day Stephen bought me a bottle of water. It was December 2011. My friend Carolyn, Stephen and I were together the night before we all left to go home for Christmas break. We were at Wal-Mart, and I became very thirsty. Not wanting to spend money on bottled water, I decided to wait until we got back to the dorms. Stephen was so kind-hearted he bought me a bottle of water. I was still clueless that he liked me at that point, but I thought it was sweet of him. I told him I would never throw away the bottle. I still have the plastic label. I honestly had no clue Stephen even liked me at that time. He was so careful not show his true feelings when we spent time together that I had no idea he wanted anything more than just friendship. Later he would tell me he had liked me from the minute he met me. Stephen later told me he had so much respect for me he wanted to do things right in regards to a dating relationship. If we were to go beyond friendship, having a God-centered relationship was especially important to him.

The next day, before I left for home for Christmas break, he put a golden dove Christmas tree ornament on the roof of my car. There was no note, but I knew it could only be from Stephen. Later on I would find out how much he enjoyed giving me surprise gifts. These acts were my first clues that Stephen Reynolds might in fact like me. I was slowly putting the pieces together. Buying the bottle of water, giving me the Christmas dove, opening doors for me, and paying special attention to me when I walked into the room—Stephen Reynolds might actually like me!

CHAPTER 3

Romans 12:9-10
Let love be genuine. Abhor what is evil; hold fast
to what is good. Love one another with brotherly
affection. Outdo one another in showing honor.

ASKING ME TO THE BANQUET

Every March, Calvary Bible College has a banquet for all the students to honor the graduating seniors. The banquet is a marvelous time for students to dress up, go someplace fancy, and take pictures. It was January 2012, nearly a month and a half since Stephen had given me the Christmas dove. One particular afternoon in January, Stephen asked me to meet him in the lobby that evening to talk about the Wolfpack. Our dormitory was four stories high. The girls were on the top two floors, and the guys were on the bottom two floors. The only co-ed place to meet was the little lobby at the front of the building.

At the time, I thought it was just the normal, "how are things going with the Wolfpack," kind of talk. When I arrived, we sat down, and he seemed rather nervous. As we talked, I noticed a couple of Stephen's friends were standing around watching Stephen, but I thought they were just joking with one another. I also noticed a big round metal cake pan, the kind with a covered lid so you could not see the cake inside. My curiosity got the best of me, so I asked Stephen what was in the pan. He told me he would show me later, so we began to talk about our day. We talked about the Wolfpack and what was going on with the girls and the guys. As our conversation began to die down, Stephen got really quiet. He began rubbing his hands nervously up and down his thighs. "Ok, man, you're acting weird!" I said as he sat there nervously.

Finally Stephen looked at me and said, "Ok, let's open up this pan." At first he let me try to open it, but I was a little nervous and couldn't figure out how to open it. He helped me unclick the lid and pull it off. Inside was a white cake with red lettering, "Will you go to the Spring Banquet with me?" On the edge of the platter lay a beautiful red rose. I was shocked! I had never gone to the Spring Banquet and had never wanted to do so. I didn't enjoy "dressing up" very much. Also, since it was significant for a guy to ask a girl to go the banquet, I hadn't wanted to falsely raise a guy's hopes of being more than friends. But it was different for me with Stephen.

I looked at Stephen, and smiling said, "Yes! Of course I'll go to the Spring Banquet with you!" Stephen smiled, and I gave him a hug. I was probably as red as the rose at that point. I guess you could say I was "happily embarrassed." Stephen's friends all came out from "hiding" and congratulated us. Afterwards I found out Stephen had been working on this banquet proposal for quite a while. At Calvary, the guys usually ask the girls in a somewhat silly yet romantic way in order to "woo" them to go to banquet with them. Often times, it signaled the start of a dating relationship between the two of them. Most guys usually asked just a few weeks before the banquet. However, Stephen had planned ahead and asked me months before the banquet. I was impressed by his early planning. I was really excited and nervous all at the same time. Stephen was different from so many other guys, and it made me interested in him. This was one of the first moments when I realized this relationship could become more than just friendship.

That night I went up to my room and told my friends, Carolyn and Jill Ann, about the banquet proposal and my acceptance of it. They were excited, but they also seemed worried. The banquet can be a romantic event at our school. They were worried because they thought Stephen had romantic feelings for me, but they thought I had no romantic feelings for him. They didn't want me to falsely raise his hopes. Honestly, at the time it was all so new to me. This was the only other instance since the dove ornament that made me become aware that Stephen Reynolds liked me. I had to think about what that could mean. However, I quickly told them I felt honored to go to the banquet with Stephen. I respected him, cherished my friendship with him, loved how much he loved God, and knew he had a good heart. There was a lot I did not know about him, but what I did know about him was good. As for the romance part, I told my friends I couldn't deny the fact he intrigued me. I was willing to start dating Stephen. But, as you'll see, we didn't start officially dating until several months later. We then celebrated by eating some of the cake Stephen had made for me. Yes, he actually made it himself. I will also add he made it sugar free, because I was avoiding sugar at the time for health reasons. What a gentleman!

VALENTINE'S DAY

Early afternoon on Valentine's Day, 2012, I was going to get some Bubble Tea with my friend Jill Ann. For those of you who don't know, Bubble Tea is a drink made of frozen black tea or green tea, syrup flavorings and large, black tapioca balls. Neither of us had dates for the day, so we decided to treat each other and go out for some fun in downtown Kansas City that afternoon. As we were walking out of the dorms, Stephen came running out from the dorms and asked if I was busy later that evening. I told him I was free, and so we scheduled our first actual date at Starbucks. Jill Ann and I went to Tea Drops, our favorite shop that sold Bubble Tea and had an enjoyable afternoon together.

That evening, Stephen and I went to Starbucks. Because it

was our first outing as just the two of us, it was a little awkward. Stephen was so nervous he hardly said anything the whole way there. I, on the other hand, either make lots of small talk when I'm nervous, or I am super quiet. On this particular night I made lots of small talk. So I chatted all the way to Starbucks. We both were so nervous I can't remember if we even got any drinks! My personality is direct and to-the-point. When Stephen asked me out on the date, but didn't say why, it made me anxious! If you're a guy reading this, you probably know what Stephen was feeling. As the girl though, I just waited for Stephen to explain what was happening. However, I waited all evening for him to bring up the reason why he asked me out that night. In my mind, you do not specifically ask a girl out on Valentine's Day for no reason!

We sat down at Starbucks and Stephen started the conversation by asking me about my life's story. Earlier he had heard my faith testimony of how I became a Christian, but he was curious to learn more about me. I gave him a more detailed story of where I grew up, what high school was like for me, what God meant to me now, and what college had meant to me so far. It seemed to ease his nerves, and he shared some of his life story as well. We both shared and laughed, reminiscing about our younger years and high school. We had some interesting similarities. We had both fallen away from God for a time in our lives. God had just recently drawn us back to Himself and had filled us with a new passion to serve Him. Starbucks was closing, so I asked Stephen to drive down an old road, my favorite road, not far from Calvary. It was my favorite road because it was curvy, and it went by fields and cattle, reminding me of my farm in South Dakota. I got homesick for those wide, open spaces a lot. That road gave me a chance to see those open spaces again. As we drove down that old road, Stephen shared his testimony of how he became a Christian, but he shared it on a much deeper level than he had done with most people. Although we both had heard some of each other's faith testimonies before, we knew much more about each other's lives after that night.

After we both shared what God had done in our lives to save us, Stephen unexpectedly parked the car as if he had something to say, but nothing happened. An awkward silence began to settle in the car. Stephen started rubbing his hands on his thighs like he had when he asked me to the banquet, but he said nothing. I tried to be patient. Still he sat silently. Then I tried to help him out by saying, "So...?" But nothing worked, and we continued to sit in horrible, awkward silence. Finally, I could not take it any longer. I looked over at Stephen and said quietly, "Stephen, why did you ask me out tonight?" A look of relief settled in his eyes, but he continued to rub his hands on his thighs. "Well, if you haven't already noticed...I really like you. But not just like a guy gets a crush on a girl. I think you're very beautiful, but you're so much more than that. I've seen how you love God more than anything else in this world. I love that about you. Your passion to serve God intrigues me. I'd like to get to know you better Katie, to pursue a relationship with you. But I want to go slowly because I want my next relationship to last. If we do have a relationship, I want it to be honoring to and blessed by God." Although I assumed Stephen was going to say, "I like you," I was amazed by his answer. He looked at me and then asked what my feelings were toward him. I looked at him, this man whom I respected so much, and answered, "To be honest, I've only had a few months to think about you in a romantic way, and it seems like you have had much longer. But I've respected you since the first time I met you. Your love for God and desire to be a man seeking after Him is evident every day. You treat all women respectfully. You are handsome, but you're also humble. What matters to me is your heart, and I love your heart. You intrigue me, Stephen, and I'd like to get to know you better too!"

Stephen and I drove back to the dorms, and he was teased immediately by his buddies. That night Stephen texted me. He thanked me for the great date and for being so honest with him. There was so much more to come in our story together, but that was the beginning of the romance between Stephen Reynolds and Katie Poindexter.

OUR FAITH STORIES

Because this was the time in our story we decided we were interested in each other, we shared our faith testimonies with each other. I would like to share them with you also.

Katie's Testimony: I grew up in rural South Dakota. For the majority of my childhood, I grew up on a farm in north-central South Dakota. My family mainly did cattle ranching with some crop farming as well. I grew up in a Christian home. My parents are Christians and taught my brother and me the truths of the Gospel of Christ. When I was 4 1/2 years old, I accepted Jesus Christ as my Savior. I continued to grow in my faith from that point in time. I had different learning experiences throughout junior high and high school that helped me continue to grow in my faith. One of the biggest experiences that shaped my life was being homeschooled all 12 school years. While in high school, I joined a summer ministry with Child Evangelism Fellowship's CYIA program during every summer in high school. I graduated from homeschooling in 2008, and in the fall, I attended Calvary Bible College. The first few years were challenging for me. I found myself following my own sinful desires yet still wanting to serve God at the same time. In the spring of 2011, my junior year at Calvary, I became repentant of the things I had done and wanted to surrender all of my life to God. By that fall semester, I was passionate about my faith in God. This was the year Stephen came to Calvary.

Stephen's Testimony: Stephen grew up in Kansas City, both the Missouri and Kansas sides, at different points. His parents are Christians, teaching their children the love of God and the way to salvation. Stephen has three siblings, two older brothers, Chris and Anthony, and one younger sister, Aundra. Stephen's family is very close-knit. Stephen grew up having great respect for his parents, looking up to his older brothers, and watching out for his little sister. He did also enjoy picking on her from time to time. His dad is a pastor and also works as a serviceman for a heating and air conditioning company. His mom works in after-school programs in the KC districts.

At age six, it was discovered that Stephen had aortic stenosis. It is a heart disease that causes narrowing in the heart's aortic valve, impeding the flow of blood to the body. When he was six years old, Stephen had open-heart surgery. By God's grace, he recuperated well and did not need another surgery as expected.

Stephen accepted Jesus Christ as his Savior when he was seven years old. He continued to grow in his relationship with God, learning what it meant to be in total surrender to God. The inability to play competitive sports because of his heart condition was very humbling for him, especially since he really liked basketball. Stephen said he learned about humility by enjoying sports events from the stands. There were times he could play, and he thoroughly enjoyed those opportunities. He trusted God and sought to find joy in all things. He graduated from high school in 2008, and in the fall, he attended Allen Community College in Iola, Kansas. He was a student there for two years and found himself being tempted to do wrong. Sometimes he even fell into the temptation instead of following God. He left the school and took a year off and turned back to God. In the fall of 2011, Stephen came to Calvary Bible College. One of his goals for attending Calvary Bible College was to grow in his relationship with Jesus.

STEPHEN'S NAME

I remember the day in March 2012, toward the beginning of our relationship, when Stephen proudly told me why he was named

Stephen Phillip Reynolds. His mom and grandmother had named him after both Stephen and Phillip from the book of Acts in the Bible. Stephen was stoned to death for proclaiming the truth of the Gospel. Phillip was known for his skills as an evangelist. Stephen Reynolds was honored to bear such names, and he was especially honored to be named after a great man who was martyred for his faith.

Before Stephen told me the meaning of his name, I used to call him "Steve" like everybody else did. After he told me the meaning of his name, I began calling him Stephen. Our friends never understood why I stopped calling him Steve and started calling him Stephen. I enjoyed using his full name and honoring the meaning of it. Stephen continued to grow in his faith and was daily dedicated to win souls for Christ. He took his names seriously. Since he was named after a great martyr and evangelist, he wanted to live his life completely for Christ.

CHAPTER 4

I John 4:7, 8
Beloved, let us love one another, for love is from God, and
whoever loves has been born of God and knows God. Anyone
who does not love does not know God, because God is love.

THE BANQUET

In March 2012, the day of the banquet arrived, and all of the girls in the dorm were literally screaming with excitement. Every year I had watched the girls get all dressed up to be escorted by their dates to the Spring Banquet, but I had never gone to the Spring Banquet. Many girls would take all afternoon to get ready. They would do their nails, hair, and makeup with their friends and hall mates. It was a big deal. As for me, I cared more about a nap that afternoon than getting all dressed up for the evening. Even after my nap, I had plenty of time to do my hair, makeup, and nails. I even had time to watch the animated version of *Beauty and the Beast*.

The theme for the banquet was a masquerade. So everyone dressed up accordingly, and many people wore masks. Our group of friends decided to simply use face paint to draw "masks" on our faces. It was pretty fun. The banquet that spring was held at a mansion by a lake with luxurious grounds to stroll through, a large water fountain to enjoy, and the interior of the mansion itself to explore. The evening included a feast of delicious food and a speaker honoring the seniors. We all enjoyed each other's company immensely. Stephen and I took our first picture together that evening. Stephen was an excellent gentleman, escorting me with his offered arm everywhere, getting me water when it was time to eat, and even pulling out my chair to seat me at the table. We both enjoyed our time and laughed a lot that night. What great memories we made! I'll always treasure the memories made that night.

MEETING HIS PARENTS

A few weeks before Easter in 2012, Stephen asked me if I would like to meet his parents. "Yes!" I exclaimed. I knew Stephen had a younger sister and two older brothers. I also knew that his dad was a pastor, and his mom worked in the school district. I was excited to meet Stephen's family and see if they had some of the same likes and characteristics as Stephen. Stephen loved sports, laughter, teasing, good food, and Jesus. I wanted to know if his family enjoyed these same things.

After Easter that spring, Stephen and I found a day when we were both available and his parents were available. They had us over for supper at their home in northern Kansas City, just 45 minutes away from Calvary Bible College. Stephen's sister Aundra was there too. Meeting Stephen's parents and Aundra was awesome. They welcomed me in and made me feel completely at home. I got a tour of their house. I watched basketball on the television with Mr. Reynolds and Stephen. Then we ate the best barbeque ribs ever. The Reynolds really know how to cook them! We talked and got to know each other with a lot of laughter during the conversation. I remember Aundra bringing out Stephen's baby pictures. She gave me one to take back to the dorms with me. I accidentally asked Mr. Reynolds how old he was. To this day he jokingly holds it against me, saying I called him old.

Mr. Reynolds is full of knowledge about God. He is passionate about people standing up for their Christian faith in the world. I respect him for that. He has such an inspirational passion for God that I don't always see in other pastors or fathers. I also discovered that Mr. Reynolds worked two other jobs besides being a pastor. I gained much more respect for his passion to preach on Sundays in addition to putting in a full week's work.

Mrs. Reynolds can cook and bake pretty much anything, and she can make some of the best cakes I've ever had. When I met her that night and found out she loved to bake, my heart swelled with more love for her. She enjoyed baking as much as I did! Mrs. Reynolds also has a strong faith and trust in God. I saw that in her that night, and it has stayed true to this day. I admire that about her. Aundra is very sweet and fun, having a great relationship with Stephen. I appreciated her right away because not everyone has a close relationship with their siblings. I could tell that she and Stephen had a close relationship with each other. My brother and I are close, and it was awesome and special to see the care and closeness they had. Aundra also has a great relationship with God, which you can see by the way she lives her life. I loved meeting the Reynolds that night, and I couldn't wait to spend more time with them in the future.

APRIL 9, 2012

It was a beautiful, warm spring night when Stephen asked me if I would go on a walk with him. "I would love too!" I said. We started walking around the campus. Then Stephen started leading me toward the school cafeteria on the opposite side of campus. As we neared the cafeteria, we also neared the area on campus the students call the "couple's bench." It was a simple bench that sat under a tree next to the cafeteria, but usually only couples would sit on it. As we neared the "couple's bench," I saw a single rose on the bench. I stopped and said, "Aw, did you put that there?" Stephen was nervous, but I hadn't noticed until now. He told me to sit down on the bench. As I sat down, I saw there was also a pink card. I picked up the rose and smelled it, smiling. I love flowers! Stephen sat next to me, but soon he nervously stood. Picking up the card he said, "I wrote you a poem." With that, he read it to me.

> *"To describe a woman like you, Where do I begin?*
> *You don't see who I was in the past; you see who I am within.*
> *When we first met, and I asked you to keep it real.*
> *You didn't hesitate to answer; you just*
> *smiled and said "I always will."*
> *That may seem small to others, but I still remember that day.*
> *Because ever since then, you've always been the same.*
> *I don't believe in rushing things, I'd rather take it slow,*
> *but this question I want to ask, you may already know.*
> *Katie, you're a Godly woman, more precious*
> *than a diamond that shines.*
> *So now I'm going to stop reading and tell you what's on my mind."*

With that, Stephen sat down on the bench and told me how he felt about me. Then he got quiet for just one second and asked, "Katie, will you be my girlfriend?" Stephen was romantic. The flower was special. The poem was sweet. But his love for God, and his effort to take the time to make the evening special was what really touched my heart. I responded excitedly, "Yes!"

Stephen explained that he had taken his time praying and asking the Lord whether or not this relationship was something he should pursue. He wanted to move slowly toward a deeper relationship than just friendship. After he took me out on Valentine's Day, I thought we would be dating soon. Little did I know his apparent "slowness" was caused by how much he sought God's will for our relationship. I loved that about Stephen, especially after I found out why he took so long to ask me to be his girlfriend. In the months leading up this special evening, Stephen had been doing a lot of praying. However, he had also asked his dad, his two brothers, his two best friends, and my two best friends for their opinions on our relationship. During those months, it was really hard for me to wait. I was confused about what was taking so long for something to change in our relationship. When he told me why he had waited so long, I could not help but have more respect for this amazing man.

Having officially become a couple, Stephen and I walked happily back to the dorms, laughing together When we got back to the dorms, all of our friends were waiting to see what had happened. Since Stephen had told his two best friends, word got around to others about the couple's bench and Stephen's asking me to be his girlfriend. Seeing our smiling faces, they knew right away that we were officially dating. There were congratulations and hugs all around. What a joyful time we had! The first few months of dating were fun, but they were also somewhat weird as we switched from being friends to dating. Stephen and I went on a few dates alone, but most of our time together was spent hanging out with our friends. When we needed time for just the two of us, we would usually go on a walk around campus. Since most of our time together for the first few months was spent hanging out with our friends, we didn't spend much quality time alone. We had a lot to learn about meeting our needs as a couple in the dating relationship ahead of us.

DATING WITH DIFFERENT HERITAGES

Where I grew up in South Dakota, the main ethnicities were Caucasian and Native American. There just weren't many African Americans there. I never imagined myself dating an African American man. I wasn't racist against them; it just wasn't something I had thought about because it wasn't the "normal" way of life that I had seen growing up. Stephen grew up in an African American family and culture. He told me he never imagined himself dating a Caucasian woman. This was not because he was racist; it was because it wasn't the normal way of life he had grown up seeing. It would have been typical for him to marry an African American woman. Although we were from different heritages, Stephen was African American and I was Caucasian, we were both proud of our heritages.

What a shock we experienced when we started dating! First, Stephen and I had to adjust to it for ourselves. The best way to explain it was that there were new experiences. Not only were we getting to know each other's personality, preferences, and families, we were getting to know each other's culture. Yes, Caucasians and African Americans are different! Each of us had gone through different experiences, and we had to respect that, learn through that, and enjoy each other's unique personality and families. It was not extremely hard for Stephen and me to date, but I want you to know challenges came our way because of the different colors of our skin. During the first few months of our relationship, we heard strangers make racist comments about us. Many people gave us odd looks if we held hands, if we looked like we were enjoying our date, if Stephen offered me his arm like a gentleman, or if Stephen did anything gentlemanly on our dates. After the first few months, we learned to ignore the rude looks and comments that came our way. Both of us thought people stopped jabbing us. In reality, we just stopped noticing because we were on "cloud nine," and we no longer cared what people thought about us.

It was a shock to both of our families when we told them we were dating. I don't believe they were against our dating. I think it was just a lot to absorb at the beginning when I was bringing home an African American man and Stephen was bringing home a Caucasian woman. It was not what our families expected for either of us. But after our families met us and got over their shock, they welcomed us with open arms!

Stephen and I did not see different skin color as a bad thing when we looked at each other. We saw a person. We loved the individual wearing the opposite skin color. There are lots of people in the world who are racist. Many racist jokes are said to different individuals. I hope that one day we will be able to look past skin color. Stephen and I prayed for that to happen in our nation. Heaven will see that dream come true. There will be no more racism or discrimination based on skin color. We will all be living together in unity as one family. I love you all, anyone reading this. It doesn't matter how you look. I'm sorry if you've experienced racism. You may say, "Katie, you don't really know what it's like." You are right. I probably don't understand, but I've had a peek. Some of the passions Stephen and I shared were trying to show love to the world and teaching the world that racism is wrong. We wanted to show people the importance of living together in unity. God created the different skin colors and loves the variety of people He put into the world. Why shouldn't we love whom He loves?

THINGS WE ENJOYED DOING TOGETHER

Stephen and I loved spending time together. We loved to laugh. Stephen was really good at making people laugh. We loved sharing joyful times together. We loved being with our closest friends. Before I got sick, we spent many days playing basketball together. Sometimes just the two of us played, and sometimes we played with friends. Although Stephen still had his heart disease, he was able to play basketball for fun if he didn't overexert himself. Even when I got sick, we still laughed and found new ways to enjoy spending time together. Life was hard, but we sought to find joy in the hard times. I loved to bake for Stephen, and he loved to eat everything I baked. It was the perfect arrangement! Stephen loved to rap for me and sing to me. It was very common on a date night to hear a spontaneous, poetic rap melody into which Stephen wove facts about our lives and relationship. We enjoyed being a couple and learning about each other. I will always remember Stephen and me laughing together on every date.

CHAPTER 5

PSALM 73:25-28
Whom have I in heaven but you?
And there is nothing on earth that I desire besides you.
My flesh and my heart may fail,
but God is the strength of my heart and my portion forever.
For behold, those who are far from you shall perish;
you put an end to everyone who is unfaithful to you.
But for me it is good to be near God;
I have made the Lord God my refuge,
that I may tell of all your works.

5 MINUTES TO LIVE

The summer of 2012 appeared to have wonderful, new things in store for both Stephen and me. However, God had very different plans for us. Each of us had signed up to do separate internships. The cool thing about our internships was that they both were in Kansas City and involved working with the homeless. Stephen signed up with City Union Mission's summer internship program working with homeless kids of inner Kansas City. He had a deep love for working with young people. One could see that he passionately desired for them to know Christ personally as their Savior and friend. My internship was for my senior counseling class. All through college, I had always held a passion for the inner city, the down-and-out individuals, and especially the homeless. Many times in my college years, I ministered to the homeless on the streets or at shelters. I signed up to do my internship at Eleos, a coffee shop located in the inner city near the homeless shelters. The employees at Eleos help the homeless by giving them backpacks full of hygiene materials and food. The employees also do many forms of evangelizing, host Bible studies, build personal relationships with people through the coffee shop, and do so much more. Stephen and I were both excited to see what God had for us to learn and do that summer.

Stephen's internship started in June, but my internship did not start until July. We hardly saw each other at the beginning of that summer because Stephen's internship kept him so busy. While Stephen was busy in June, I prepared for my internship and also enjoyed the summer with friends. I truly missed Stephen, but I was thankful for the ability to be surrounded by my friends before my internship started.

The first day of my internship was quite surreal. It was one of those experiences that is nearly impossible to describe how it felt. As I walked in the door that first day, I was so nervous and asked God for His peace. During my first day, I learned about the coffee shop, cleaned the coffee shop, and acquainted myself with the people that worked there. I also went on a prayer walk with the founder of Eleos and another gentleman. During the prayer walk, we walked around neighborhoods asking people on the street if they needed a backpack or a bottle of water on that hot July day. We also asked people if we could pray for them. Many people accepted the opportunity for prayer. It was amazing to see so many touching things in just one day. I knew I would continue to see wonderful things every day of my internship. I was so excited to see God working through this ministry!

The next week was hot and muggy. Something happened which I never planned. I became sick. That week I had to call Eleos and tell them that I was too sick to come in for my internship. On

Thursday night of my week of sickness, I started having trouble breathing. (I think it was the second week in July.) I had been diagnosed with asthma a few years earlier, so I grabbed my inhaler. I took a few puffs and waited for the medicine to take effect, but nothing happened. I drank a full cup of water thinking the water might help me. Breathing continued to be difficult. I went outside hoping the fresh air would help, but I only became worse and stumbled my way back inside my apartment. I lay down on the couch, grabbed my phone and texted four friends who were EMTs, asking for their advice. My friends who texted back said to call an ambulance. However, I grew up never really going to the hospital. I hadn't needed emergency medical help before in life. I really didn't think I needed an ambulance now, so I ignored their advice. Then my friend Katie, who was one of the EMTs I had texted, called me. I remember muttering some answers to her. Then I heard Katie say she was calling an ambulance.

The next thing I remember is lying on the couch and taking a short breath. I tried to take another breath, but I could not. Then I passed out. As I lay unconscious, I had a vision of talking to God. He said to me, "Katie, you have five minutes to live. If the ambulance does not get here in the next five minutes, you're coming home to Heaven. Are you ready?" My heart broke. "No, God!" I cried. "What about Stephen? How can I leave him like this? What about my friends? Or my family, God? Plus, there's so much I want to do for Your glory. Is it really my time to go home?" With every question I asked, God gently responded, "I have everything in control. I will take care of them." It was a very difficult conversation for me. Life was so good, and I was enjoying it. I wanted to stay on earth. However, at the end of our conversation, I was ready to accept going to Heaven. During our conversation, God helped me understand my life is all about Him. It's not about my wants. (John 12:24-25). God then said, "Katie, there are two minutes left." The vision ended, and I slowly became more aware of my surroundings. I heard the fire fighters break down the door of my apartment and the EMTs come in with an oxygen tank. I never fully stopped breathing, so they didn't have to perform CPR. But they gave me five tanks of oxygen before I started breathing normally again.

The ambulance took me to the ER. The doctors discovered the reason I was having trouble breathing was because my apartment was full of black mold, and I was having a severe allergic reaction to it. I could see the black mold climbing the walls of the bathroom and the hallway. They told me to move out of the apartment as soon as possible. I had only been living in my apartment for two months. After my trip to the ER, I returned to my apartment for one week before I moved in with a sweet family, the Surgeon family. During that week, I stayed with some friends for a few days. I spent the rest of the week in my apartment with a friend who kept an eye on me. My health was very sensitive, and my energy level was very low after the allergic reaction to the black mold. With a heavy heart, I canceled my internship. I hoped to get better after a month of recovery at the Surgeon's house, but my physical condition stayed the same. After spending four weeks with the Surgeon family, I moved back to the dorms on campus. Only a month after moving back to the dorms, my health became worse.

The night I nearly stopped breathing marked the beginning of a very long journey of health issues and questions that I still deal with today. However, that particular night was full of blessings I want to share with you. First, Katie was a blessing for calling the ambulance. I'm so thankful for her awareness and action despite my unwillingness to call an ambulance. Second, my friends who followed the ambulance and were with me in the ER were a blessing of support. Lastly, I called Stephen later that night, after I returned from the ER. I explained all that had happened, including the vision. As we talked, I cried when we both said, "God is good!" at the same time. We did not have to explain what that meant to us; we both had a new, clear understanding of who God is to us. God felt nearer and more important than ever before in our lives. We knew God was good. We realized He had given me life, not just once at birth but again when He saved my life as I lay in my apartment. When we said, "God is good," we truly meant it, and it was a wonderful blessing to share that understanding with each other.

The rest of the summer went very differently than I thought it would go. Stephen and I did not see much of each other. He was 45 minutes away from me and was busy with his internship. A week after my near-death experience, he was able to come and see how I was doing. I know he was very concerned about me, but at the time, he seemed torn between wanting to be at his internship and wanting to take care of me. In my heart, I was torn as well. I did not want Stephen to stop doing ministry, but I felt very uncared for by him. I really did not feel like we were in a dating relationship. I felt like I was just his friend. We had only dated two months before his internship started. In those two months, we did not spend much quality time together since we were still figuring out how to go from being friends to dating. Stephen went back to his internship after his short visit, and I remained with the Surgeon family. All summer long, we hardly talked or spent much time together. Fear began to rear its ugly head. I began to wonder, *If Stephen is more passionate about ministry than his family and me, then how can I keep dating him?* It broke my heart to think those thoughts, but it didn't change the fact that they were there. I'm sure other girls can relate to what was running through my head. I loved Stephen, and I knew he cared for me. But if Stephen wanted to be all into ministry, I wondered if we should end our dating relationship.

At the end of his internship, which was also the end of the summer, I drove to meet him and talk with him. I was so broken that I couldn't stop crying on and off during my drive. I thought I was going to have to break up with him because he didn't take our relationship seriously. I felt like a third wheel in his life. We went on a date to Cracker Barrel, and then we went to a park to talk. Stephen could see something was wrong. The two of us were coming from completely different summer experiences. Stephen was fully energized having just experienced the most amazing summer of his life doing ministry for God. I was fully drained having spent my summer with friends taking care of me and spending time with me while I was sick. Stephen was hardly around me that summer. I want you all to know I don't blame Stephen for feeling so energized by his internship. Honestly, if I had been able to do my internship, I would probably have felt the same way.

While we were at the park, Stephen asked me what was wrong. My broken heart could not take it any longer. I started to sob. Stephen was shocked and asked, "Are you alright, Baby?" I looked at him and shook my head. Then I cleared my tears and began to speak. "Stephen, I feel so far from you. I don't feel as if we are in a dating relationship at all. We haven't built up any form of a relationship all summer long. Since I've become sick, I don't feel that you even care about me. It feels like your ministry has been more of a priority than our relationship. I feel torn because doing ministry is important to me too, but I don't know where that leaves me in your life." As I talked, I drew an illustration on a napkin.

This is how I believe Stephen and I and all believers should be living their lives.

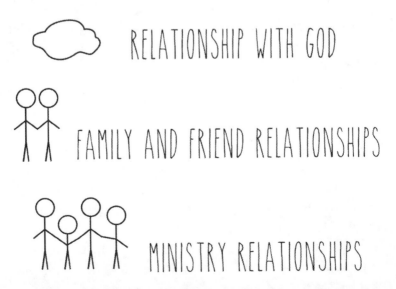

RELATIONSHIP WITH GOD

FAMILY AND FRIEND RELATIONSHIPS

MINISTRY RELATIONSHIPS

I shared my heart with Stephen. "The beginning of the summer was hard, and I found other things to fill my void. I finally realized that only by putting God first would that void be filled. I asked God to forgive me for placing other things before Him in my life. It was on the night I struggled to breathe that I realized I needed to strive to keep God first."

Stephen sat on the hood of the car processing everything I had said. I think I scared him, humbled him, and impacted him with God's truth all in just ten minutes. I had no intention of lecturing my boyfriend or hurting him. I truly wanted to talk out the issue and hopefully be able to resolve the problem we had. I sat next to him silently allowing him to process what I had said. After a few minutes had gone by, Stephen took the napkin that had my drawing on it and said, "You've had a lot more time to think about this than I have. But I see the truth in what you're saying. All summer long, I've put ministry first before God and before you, my family and my friends. I'm slowly beginning to see the affects it's having on my relationships with all of you. I cannot say that I regret doing the ministry, but I'm sorry for hurting you and my family and friends. May God forgive me for not putting Him first in my ministry."

I'd love to tell you from that moment on things were easy for us. I'd love to say dating was a breeze! But I would be lying. There was a lot of forgiveness and healing that lay ahead of us in our relationship. We needed to learn how to communicate more effectively and to be more intentional in growing our friendship. We learned a lot that day. We both learned we had to keep God at the center of our relationship in order to keep a well-balanced, godly relationship. We also learned we had to communicate our needs to each other. Lastly, we learned we were going to hurt each other and let each other down. We needed to learn how to forgive, love, and heal in our relationship. Because we had such different summer experiences, it forced us to learn the valuable lessons of needing to be closer together as a couple, learning to communicate, and spending time getting to know each other more. When we went back to college that fall, we were more intentional in our dating relationship.

CHAPTER 6

Job 1:21
And he [Job] said, "Naked I came from my mother's womb, and naked shall I return. The Lord gave, and the Lord has taken away; blessed be the name of the Lord."

THE BOOK OF JOB

Stephen and I had the most wonderful dates. They were not "normal," but they were always very special to us. We truly enjoyed every moment together. I'll be honest with you. We had hard times and difficult days in our relationship. Like all couples, we had to work to keep our relationship healthy. But God always helped us, and when we kept Him as the center of our relationship, our relational issues were always resolved.

After I got sick, it was really hard for us to find a new normal for our relationship. Oh, many times I pleaded with God to send me a book to explain how to live my life and to make it easier to understand how life worked when you were sick! Some days I told Stephen, "If only there was a book on 'How to Live Your Life When You're Sick and in a Dating Relationship' then my life would be much easier." Stephen and I would sometimes laugh at the idea of someone writing a book on how to live our lives. On other days, however, we were very serious, and I would be moved to tears. Life was so hard! Being sick was a hard enough trial. But being sick and being in a serious dating relationship was an even harder trial. Our knowledge of dating was turned upside down. We could not do all the things normal people did. Both of us struggled in many areas. Stephen struggled with knowing how to lead me spiritually. Because I was sick, he had to lead me in different ways at different times. He had to be very gentle with me spiritually. I struggled with letting Stephen lead me through different areas in my life and through my sickness. I also really struggled with bitterness and frustration at God for my sickness. For some reason, my sickness always seemed to get in the way of everything I ever wanted. At this time in my life, especially, it seemed to get in the way of my relationship with Stephen. It was very hard.

Eventually I got to a point where I could thank God for His mercy and goodness in the midst of my sickness. He helped me realize that complaining wouldn't fix my problems. God showed me that even if I never got well, I needed to let Him change my heart's attitude toward my sickness. But it was a long journey getting to the point of allowing God to change my heart.

After I had been sick for five months, Stephen suggested we read through the book of Job together. Stephen and I related with the life of Job in the Bible. We both took to heart every word from the book of Job. Job went through some very hard things in his life. They were actually terrible things. We started reading in October 2012, and finished near the beginning of December 2012. At first, we started reading a chapter every morning together at breakfast. But after a month, I felt so depressed by Job's life because it seemed to be repeated in my own life I told Stephen I could not handle reading Job anymore. We sat down to talk about it and decided we had to finish reading the book of Job together. We were over halfway through the book, and Stephen and I both didn't like leaving something unfinished. So, we decided to finish reading Job.

One beautiful day at the beginning of December 2012, Stephen and I went to a pretty little park and parked the car. It was cold outside, so we sat in the car with open Bibles. We decided to start at the beginning of Job and read all the way through it. For three or four hours, I cannot quite remember how long it took us, we sat there, side by side, reading the book of Job aloud, alternating between us. When we read the account of the hard times in Job's life, I sat and cried as Stephen read. Sometimes I interrupted and explained why I felt like Job in my situation. We read how Job's friends didn't seem to be helpful or to understand what he was going through. I remember crying, putting my head on Stephen's shoulder and saying, "Stephen, this is how I feel. I have nothing against my friends or family. But I can relate to Job, and no one can relate to me." He held me and let me cry. He knew I was hurting, and I felt alone. Stephen was such a patient man. I am so thankful for him. God placed him in my life for so many reasons.

When I got done crying, Stephen said, "Baby, I know I don't understand, but I wish I did. I wish I could take away your pain. I know that's not God's plan, but I pray that I could take your pain away every day. I hope you know that I'll try my best to help and understand as best as possible." It is interesting how God put Stephen and me together because Stephen and I were alike in many ways. One large similarity was the fact that we cared more about each other's wellbeing than our own wellbeing. I'd rather lose my arm than watch Stephen lose his arm, but Stephen would rather lose his arm than see me lose my arm.

One thing that stuck with Stephen and me the whole time we were reading through Job that afternoon was in Job 1:21. "Naked I came from my mother's womb, and naked shall I return. The Lord gave, and the Lord has taken away; blessed be the name of the Lord." Job never gave up his faith in God. He continued to praise God even when trials and hard times came upon him. At the end of his story, God richly blessed Job. If you read the entire book of Job and aren't amazed by our good God, keep reading the Bible until you see how good He is! Stephen and I learned so much through our afternoon read that day. We knew many trials and hard days were yet to come upon us. However, we realized that day was special. It was a breakthrough for us. We realized that God is faithful yesterday, today and, tomorrow. Trials can draw us closer to God. If we would let Him, God could use these trials we were facing for good in our lives.

The lesson I was beginning to learn that day and will continue to remember for the rest of my life is that God is in control. God gives me everything I have. He gives me my life, the air I breathe, my family, food, clothing, and He gave me Stephen. I am blessed! Counting my blessings has become a daily and hourly habit for me now. I am moved to tears by the countless blessings that arrive in my life each day, and all I can do is say, "Thank you, Lord, thank you, Lord, thank you, Lord." I AM BLESSED!

ROCKS ON THE SIDEWALK

On a cold January day in 2013, I awakened to the sound of my phone ringing. I looked to see who was calling and saw it was Stephen. As I sleepily said, "Hello," I looked at the clock and saw that it was around 2:00 P.M. Stephen was leaving for work, and he wanted to see me before he left. I was in the dorms, not feeling well that day. (I was still dealing with health issues after my reaction to mold. At this point, the doctors didn't know what wrong with my health. That is the reason I simply call it my sickness. I will explain more about my health journey in later chapters.) I sat on my bed as we talked on the phone. Then Stephen told me to look out my window. Some days when I was unable to leave my room, I would wave goodbye to him from my dorm room on the 4th floor as we talked on the phone. I walked over to my window and looked down. As I looked outside, I saw that Stephen had used rocks on the sidewalk to outline the words, "Black Steve loves Katie." (He used a heart shape in place of the word "love." There were four Stephens in the dorms. Stephen was the only African American named Stephen. He clarified that he was the one who loved me by using the word "black," so everyone would know it was him!)

Then I saw Stephen smiling very broadly, looking up at me, and waving. It was the sweetest thing I could ever wake up to see. I waved back, and we talked for a few more minutes before he had to go to work. The best thing about this sweet act was that the rocks stayed on the sidewalk for quite a long time, and I was able to wake up and see his message every day.

CHAPTER 7

James 1:2-4
*Count it all joy, my brothers, when you meet trials of various
kinds, for you know that the testing of your faith produces
steadfastness. And let steadfastness have its full effect,
that you may be perfect and complete, lacking in nothing.*

COUNT YOUR BLESSINGS

By January 2013, I had been sick for almost seven months. I
continued to get sicker and weaker as the weeks passed. It had
been a long journey for Stephen and me as a dating couple. We
had to endure the raging storm that blew around us every second
of every day during my sickness. God created both Stephen and me
with positive outlooks on life. Together, we fought the good fight
of keeping our faith alive and well. But, it was a hard journey for
both of us, and I became weary trying to keep my positive attitude.

I tried to keep my hopes up, have a good attitude, and
believe God had everything in control. Yet, I slowly began to
give in to discouragement. I started to feel sorry for myself. The
discouragement started to sink in, and hopelessness began to
overtake my normally positive attitude. At the start of my sickness,
Stephen and I had begun to say, "God is good, and life is hard,"
but that wasn't enough to give me hope anymore.

I fought this sadness for a few weeks until one day Stephen

and I went on a date to get fried chicken at Popeyes. We got into the car, and I started to complain. How I wished I could play basketball with him, or hang out in a crowd without feeling sick, or stop seeing double all the time. I had even stopped driving my car due to vision issues. On and on I complained. All the way to Popeyes, Stephen drove silently, listening to me. We got to the drive-thru and ordered our food. Then all of the sudden, Stephen started singing at the top of his lungs,

"COUNT YOUR BLESSINGS
NAME THEM ONE BY ONE;
COUNT YOUR BLESSINGS
SEE WHAT GOD HAS DONE;
COUNT YOUR BLESSINGS
NAME THEM ONE BY ONE;
COUNT YOUR MANY BLESSINGS
SEE WHAT GOD HAS DONE."

We had just sung that song in church that previous Sunday. His singing made me stop my complaining like I had gotten a slap from the Lord. As much as I didn't want to admit it, I realized God was using Stephen to remind me to count my blessings. Then all of the sudden, Stephen started counting to ten with a huge grin on his face. He turned and looked at me, "Sweetheart, you better start naming your blessings, one by one." In my heart I knew he was right, but I was prideful and selfish. I honestly didn't want to be thankful, so I firmly told him, "No." There was sadness in his eyes. He started counting again with a smile and twinkle in his eyes, "1, 2, 3, 4, 5, 6, 7, 8, 9, 10. Baby, God wants you to be thankful. Will you count your blessings?" There were tears in my eyes, so much hurt, so much pain. Stephen understood my hardships. He understood my struggle and how difficult it was to lose the things I loved. I was angry about losing my health. I didn't want to count my blessings. We got our food and parked the car. I began to cry and say, "I am thankful for...." I counted about 50 blessings that night. It was the beginning of the emotional healing process for me, releasing my anger toward God for my sickness.

Today I can say I am thankful for the many things I learned while going through this sickness. I can also say I am so thankful for Stephen who was such a patient man. He took great care of me and was a spiritual leader to me. Most of all, I am thankful for a God who never gives up on His children during hard days and struggles.

Although I am still learning how to faithfully practice it, I can say I know what it is like to count my blessings in the midst of the trials I face. By recognizing these blessings, I recognized many other blessings. I even discovered true joy in the midst of the trials. The trials didn't go away, but I found joy in the middle of them by counting my many blessings. In the Bible, the book of James talks about enduring trials and counting it all joy when we face trials. I have learned to find joy in the midst of the trials. (James 1:2-4) All the way home from Popeyes, Stephen and I were filled with joy and sang at the top of our lungs the hymn "Count Your Blessings." Even now as I think about that night, I am humbled, thankful, and unable to keep from smiling from the joy that swells within my heart while recalling such a great memory. God is good!

PRAYERS UPON PRAYERS

Prayer became a large and truly vital aspect of my life when the trials of my sickness started coming. The same can also be said for Stephen's life. As a couple, we had our strongest moments when we stopped to pray together, sought the Lord's will, and got on our knees in prayer. We were completely humbled because we realized that God is God and without Him we are nothing. We were often reminded of our need for His help in our lives. There are so many memories of times when Stephen and I both went to God asking for His help. We rejoiced together when we watched Him give us the help we needed. Stephen was the leader in our relationship. Almost every time we were together, we prayed together, and he normally led us in prayer. Sometimes they were simple, short prayers. Other times, we would spend quality time praying about the things on our hearts. Prayer is having a conversation with God, and that is what we did in those times. We told God what was on our hearts and asked for His help and guidance.

Whenever Stephen and I would get in the car to go somewhere, Stephen would pray under his breath or even grab my hand and pray for safe travels. Whether we drove far away or a mile away, Stephen always prayed for safe travels. Even when I wasn't in the car, he would still say a prayer for safe travels. Stephen would sit in his car for a minute or two, with his head bowed, before driving away. If you didn't know he was praying, you'd think something was wrong, or he was taking his time driving away. In those moments, Stephen was actually praying.

Sometimes, if I looked extremely sick, I would notice a worried look in Stephen's eye, and he would pray over me and my sick body. Sometimes he would pray for me, and other times we would go before God together with our plea for Him to heal my body of the sickness that plagued me. As much as we wanted me to get well quickly, I think deep down I knew I was going to be sick for at least a few years. I told Stephen about my intuition. With that intuition, yet not wanting to give up hope for my healing, we continued to pray for my immediate healing every day for about a year. There is nothing the Lord cannot do, but I believe sometimes He allows us to go through hard things in life to help mature us. Maturity in faith and in life is not gained by walking the easy road.

My family, friends, and especially Stephen struggled to watch me go through the pain of sickness. It is never easy to watch someone you love go through hard times. As I lived through my sickness then and even now continue to live through this sickness, I have my ups and downs and many hard days, but with God as my rock, my faith remains firm.

CHAPTER 8

I Corinthians 13:4-7
Love is patient and kind; love does not envy or boast;
it is not arrogant or rude. It does not insist on its own
way; it is not irritable or resentful; it does not rejoice at
wrongdoing, but rejoices with the truth. Love bears all things,
believes all things, hopes all things, endures all things.

RED ROSES

Stephen was romantic. On every date or special occasion, he bought me a rose. Sometimes he bought multiple roses. Sometimes he would put the rose on the car seat for me to see once I got in the car. Other times, he would be holding the rose in his hands, waiting to give it to me. Another way he liked to give me a rose was by putting the stem in his mouth and waiting for me to take it out. He was a character! I would always laugh whenever he put the rose in his mouth. Sometimes I didn't know what to do with him because he was so playful. He would do silly and unexpected things that made me laugh. Every time he gave me the rose, he would smile the most gigantic smile you could ever see on a person's face. We would leave for our date smiling and laughing. I saved every rose he ever gave me. I dried each one and have them all in two glass jars on my bookcase.

CHAPTER 8

SUNRISES AND SUNSETS

Stephen and I loved to watch the sunrises and sunsets. Some days, when I was able, we would wake up early and drive into the country. We would find a country road and get out of the car to sit and watch the sunrise. Other days we would drive to another random destination and park, watching the sunset and seeing the marvelous, beautiful colorful scene which God painted before our eyes. We would sit in awe of our awesome God who created such a beautiful masterpiece.

HOW WE SHOWED LOVE TO EACH OTHER

Romantic walks, date nights, and long talks continued to flow through and prosper during Stephen's and my relationship. Although many hardships came our way, we found ways to enjoy each other, to get to know each other on a deeper level, and to discover there were still things we did not know about each other. Laughter or smiles found their way into almost every moment of our time together. We learned to find the joy in simple moments. We enjoyed the times when Stephen took me to class escorting me like a gentleman. It was very sweet and also very practical for him to do that for me. At that point, I was so dizzy all the time I actually needed to hold his arm to help me walk. We even learned to cherish the times when we were in need and got on our knees, praying to our Heavenly Father for help. Praying together was very special to us.

The first time Stephen preached during chapel at Calvary was a great day! I sat there so proud of the man God was making him to be. He stood behind the chapel pulpit, in March 2013, nervous yet excited to share what God was teaching him. It may not be surprising to you, dear reader, that he preached a sermon on trusting God through hard times.

There were also times when we did special acts of service

to bless people we did not even know. This was one our favorite things to do on date nights. I now smile at the memories. Stephen and I would drive around and pick a random car and park next to it. Then we would pull out a notebook and start writing a letter. The letter would tell our story. Even though we were going through a hard time with my sickness, God was still a good God. We wrote about whatever we were going through right then and there, and we would add a scripture that gave us hope. We would always end our letter by writing, "Whether you believe in God, you're seeking to, or you do not know Him at all, we prayed for you tonight." Then we would pray for the person who owned the vehicle. After we prayed together, Stephen would get out, fold up the piece of paper, and put it on the windshield, and we would drive away. Some nights we did more than one car. Some days we teared up as we prayed. One night we found a K-Love company vehicle and left a message telling our story and asking them to pray for us. (K-Love is a Christian radio station that Stephen and I enjoyed listening to together in Kansas City.) Most of all, God encouraged us as we went around blessing strangers. It was also fun and exhilarating! Sometimes we would laugh and invent stories about what people would think when they came out to read our letters. But in the end, we left the cars knowing we were sharing who God was and what He was doing in our lives. Even in the hard times, God is still good.

Stephen and I were dedicated to putting the other person before our personal needs and wants. Isn't that what marriage is supposed to be like? As Stephen and I grew as a couple, we grew in our love for each other and in our knowledge of what a true, God-centered relationship should be like. We continued seeking God and trying to put Him first in everything. However, we were not perfect. We messed up many times. We had squabbles, disagreements, and arguments, yet we continued to try and seek God's help to resolve those issues. Notice how I said "try." We are humans, just like you. Though we are sinful, human, and very imperfect, we tried to do right. Because we are Christians, the Holy Spirit communicated to us when we were wrong and helped keep us on the right path. When the Holy Spirit works in your heart, it's powerful and humbling.

God continued to grow us closer to Him and closer to each other. It was wonderful but also very hard. If someone ever tells you that relationships are easy, well, I wouldn't believe them! Relationships are hard, but they are worth it, especially good, healthy relationships. In a dating relationship, when preparing for marriage, the two individuals start becoming "one." It's awesome and difficult at the same time. Changes have to be made. Emotions are crazy. Perspectives change, and so much more is happening all at the same time. Stephen and I enjoyed getting to know each other, but it was also a hard process. As we got to know each other more, excitement grew as the talk of marriage began. I remember we would both giggle with excitement at the prospect of spending more time together after we were married. We found new marriage-related topics to discuss. I now know why premarital counseling is a good idea. There is so much to think about before getting married! I have wondered if my being so sick put additional stress on our marriage planning that might not otherwise have been there.

My sickness progressed, and my body was so weak that I was sleeping 15 to 20 hours a day. As you can imagine, that caused a lot of mental stress for me as I thought about the possibility of our marriage. Thoughts began running through my mind. *How am I going to be a good wife? Will he continue to love me if we marry? I cannot clean the house. I cannot make him meals. How will I even be able to satisfy him in his needs? What will I even be able to do for him? He will be working with his heart and soul to provide for me, but I will be so sick that I won't be able to do anything for him.* As those thoughts ran through my mind day after day, a day came when Stephen and I had a talk.

By March 2013, we had been dating for 11 months. Stephen

sensed that I seemed "off." He took me for a walk in the park, and we had a nice long chat about my stressful thoughts. I told him everything that you just read, my fears of not being able to be a good wife and not being able to satisfy him. Stephen responded, "Sweetheart, if you had the heart and the health of a lion I know you would be doing all those things, but I don't need you to do any of those things." I looked at him in utter shock and confusion and began to cry. "What do you mean, Stephen? What am I supposed to do as your wife then? Just be sick?" Stephen looked at me, grabbed a tissue from his pocket and began to wipe away my tears even as more tears came. He looked me in the eye as we sat on the park bench and said with a grin, "I want you to be YOU, my Vanilla Wafer. And I want you to continue doing what you've been doing for me all this time you've been sick, and we've been dating. That to me is what I need." (Stephen and I liked giving each other pet names. "Vanilla Wafer" was one he gave me, and I loved it.) I began to cry again. He held me and let me cry as I leaned my head on his shoulder, and tears ran down my face. I was humbled. All I had been doing for Stephen since I had gotten sick was praying for him every day, talking to him on the phone at night, always ending those calls in prayer, and spending a few hours together when I was able, which was normally once a week. That didn't feel like enough to me, but it was enough for Stephen.

One thing that encouraged Stephen and me in our relationship was our love and dedication to each other. Near the start of our relationship, when Stephen shared his testimony with me, he was very open and honest about his past. You see, God's children aren't perfect. When Stephen fell away from God for a few years, he lost something very precious to him, his virginity. Whenever he talked about it, he had a sad look in his eyes. I low he wished he had waited and kept his virginity. He was so humbled and sorry for what he had done. I saw tears in his eyes when he told me about the hard times he had experienced and his actions when he had walked away from God for a few years. But God is a good and forgiving God who rescues and restores His children. Stephen was awed by God's grace and forgiveness in his life.

Stephen already knew my story. I had fallen away from God too, but I had chosen other sinful things in which to indulge myself. I was still a virgin and had never even been romantically kissed. I was saving myself for my husband. When Stephen finished sharing his testimony, he looked at me and waited to see if I still viewed him with respect, knowing he had lost his virginity. I looked at him and told him honestly what I thought. "Stephen, whether you believe me or not is your choice, but I view you the same way God does. Your past is your past. You have been redeemed. I don't like that you committed that sin, but I don't condemn you for it. I respect you even more because you asked God for forgiveness and have been given God's grace. I love you even more because you were honest and told me about your past and how hard it was for you." Stephen was amazed that I still loved him after what he had done. Stephen's present life was more important to me that his past mistakes. I told him since God has redeemed him he should live like it! Stephen was in total shock. All throughout our dating, he would bring it up and say, "I'm not a virgin, could you really love me?" Every time, I would look him in the eye and say, "I love you for who you are. You are redeemed. You are not the man from your past, and I love you even more because of your humility." Eventually, Stephen truly did believe I loved him no matter what he had done in his past. That was one of the ways I was able to show love and dedication to Stephen.

I experienced Stephen's love and dedication to me in different way. As you have read, I was sick nearly a year while dating Stephen. It was the most wonderful, humbling, and hardest experience of my life. My sickness brought new fears, hard times, and life changes. One thing I knew during my sickness was that God was using my sickness to take away my pride and humble me. There were times when I thought I had finally gotten to a point of humility in my life. Then God would gently show me new areas in my heart and life that were still prideful. Gently, He would ask me to let Him humble me even more. It was hard to say, "Yes," to that request, but I'm grateful I did. I'm still learning more about God, pride, and humility to this day.

And Stephen, dear Stephen, stayed with me through it all. His love, dedication, and grace to me during my sickness proved he was a good and faithful man. Even today, there are times I still tear up at the beautiful memories of his care for me. Stephen never left me during the hard times of my sickness. There were times I asked him why he stayed with me. Why would he love a broken, sick girl? His response was just like the response I always gave him when he would ask how I could love a man who had lost his virginity. Stephen would say, "Because of who you are, Baby. You will get better. And even if you don't, this sickness has not taken your faith in God. You still say every day that God is good. That is why I love you!" Just like it took Stephen awhile to believe the reality of my love for him, it took me about seven or eight months to truly believe that he loved me, sick or healthy. He really loved me. The reality of our love for each other hit us both around the same time. When the reality of love hit us, we both were filled with joy, God's joy. We knew our relationship was God-blessed. That day we thanked God, praised Him, and prayed for His will to be done for the rest of our lives. Little did we know what God's sovereign and perfect plan looked like for our lives.

A GODLY MAN

During spring break in March 2013, we went to my house. I really wanted to visit my grandparents on my dad's side while we were home. My grandparents lived about an hour away from my family's farm. On the day that my parents, Stephen, and I were going to go visit my grandparents, I was feeling rather sick. I was really disappointed and upset that I wouldn't be able to see my grandparents. I spent time reading my Bible and praying in my room. After a while, I went into the kitchen where my parents and Stephen were preparing to leave. I told them the sad news that I wouldn't be able to go because I was not feeling well. Normally, Stephen was my number one nurse, staying with me and taking care of me when he could. Instead, he took me aside and told me, "I would really like to meet your grandfather, and this might be my only time to meet him." Then he took my hand, looked me in the eyes and added, "Sweetheart, I cannot stay here alone with you. My flesh is too weak. I don't want to put myself in a position of looking like I'm doing something that is wrong in our dating relationship, and I think it would be best for both of us for me to go." Wow! What an honorable man! I loved Stephen and respected him. I smiled and told him to have fun. I gave him a hug and waved to him and my parents as they left for the day.

Even though it was daytime, Stephen didn't want to be alone in the house with me, especially for so long. You may think he was crazy. You may think he was being overly careful. But I appreciated the fact that the man I was dating was consciously keeping our relationship pure. He wasn't perfect, but he strove to be a godly man. He knew what his weaknesses were, and he tried not to place himself in positions that would give him the opportunity to fall into sin. He also didn't want others to think he was allowing himself to be put into those kinds of positions. Our relationship was precious to him, and he wanted to keep it pure to honor God.

ONE YEAR ANNIVERSARY

Stephen planned to propose to me on our one-year anniversary of dating. The date was April 9, 2013, and he had everything planned in his mind. He even talked to some of our friends about his idea, and they were ready to help him. Stephen had gone to my farm with me for our spring break three weeks earlier. He had ample opportunities to ask my dad for permission to marry me, but he got scared and did not ask. Stephen always regretted his indecision.

On April 8, Stephen called my dad asking for permission to marry me. Here is a quick side story about how Stephen got my dad's phone number. As we were leaving my house after spring break, Stephen suddenly opened the car door and told me he would be right back. He went into the house and asked my parents for their phone number. Mom told me about this a few days after we went back to school that week.

During their phone conversation in April, my dad explained to Stephen that he wanted to speak with him in person about this decision. Dad was worried about my health and wanted to discuss it with Stephen. Stephen respected his wish and asked if he could drive up to South Dakota that very day. Stephen and about five of his guy friends were willing to make the trip to South Dakota and return to Missouri in 24 hours so that Stephen could propose on April 9. However, there was bad weather in South Dakota at the time. Dad told Stephen to wait until graduation, which was four weeks away. Then they could talk in person.

Stephen respected my dad's wishes and waited even though he really wanted to propose to me on April 9. I knew none of this information at the time. Stephen wanted to keep the proposal a secret. I learned about all of this later from Stephen's two best friends, Stephen Buller and Troy Fraiser. However, I had suspected that Stephen was going to ask my dad if he could marry me. I thought Stephen would ask my dad during spring break, but when we left my house, I knew he hadn't asked. You know how you can "read" the people you love? I knew by Stephen's behavior that he hadn't asked my dad yet.

When the day of our one-year anniversary arrived, Stephen was full of emotions. Stephen escorted me to class as I held his arm. I could tell something was wrong, but when I asked what was wrong he told me everything was fine. It irked me to know he was not telling me why he was so upset, but I respected his decision not to tell me. That evening, we went on a walk, and I knew Stephen was still upset. Sadly, we ended up getting into a squabble. Stephen wanted me to be happy on our walk, but I could not be happy when I was seeing him so upset. Therefore, we both got upset. Couples are so confusing aren't they? I laugh now, but at the time it was not funny!

Stephen finally told me what was really bothering him. He had wanted to propose to me that day, but my dad had asked him to wait. He looked so miserable when he told me everything. I wanted to give him a hug, but even a hug was not enough to help Stephen's feelings. We sat down on a bench and just stared at the stars together. Finally, we decided we needed to pray. With heads bowed low and tears flowing from my eyes, we prayed to our Father who had been there for us in many happy times and many hard times. We finished, and I gave Stephen a long hug. I whispered in his ear, "I'm going to say, 'Yes.' " Stephen smiled very broadly, and we both laughed as we walked back to the dorms. I knew Stephen was still going to ask my dad in person for permission to marry me. I also knew Stephen was still going to do an actual proposal with a ring. Stephen was romantic, and I understood why he wanted to propose on this day. It was a special day for us. It was the same date as the day we had started dating, April 9, 2012. So, April 9, 2013, became a special day from that point on because it was the day Stephen wanted to propose.

CHAPTER 9

Psalm 62:1-2
For God alone my soul waits in silence;
from him comes my salvation.
He alone is my rock and my salvation,
my fortress; I shall not be greatly shaken.

THE NIGHT STEPHEN DIED

I wish to tell you a story,
Of a couple amazed by glory,
They were nothing without their God,
But he raised them up children of praise.
They went through many hard times,
But their prayer is what held them fast.
They prayed to their God,
"Oh, God, help us."
Their God answered their prayers,
It may not have always been what they wanted,
But their God never stopped amazing them,
His glory remained supreme.
So in the end of the story one thing remains:
You must remember to pray to the Father of all things;
He will always be of help.
But remember: his answers are best and his ways are best.

The couple in the end had a different ending than most,
It is not Disney's "Happily Ever After"
But it is God's "Perfect Plan" which is BEST!

Written by Katie, spring 2014

This poem expresses my heart regarding the events of Saturday, April 27, 2013. Although April 27, 2013 will forever be one of the hardest days of my life, God never left my side.

Stephen and I considered every moment together as a blessing from God. Because I was so sick, many times I was not able to go outside or even get out of my dorm room. It was difficult for Stephen and me to go on dates, to be together, or even to just "be" a couple. Yet, whenever we were together, we cherished every second we had.

On April 27, 2013, I was feeling really ill. I had slept most of the day. Around evening time, I was tired of being in the dorm and really missed Stephen. So Stephen and I decided to go on a short drive for some quality time together. Driving became one of the things Stephen and I did a lot together since I became sick. My body was so weak and unable to do much else. Driving on my favorite roads or going to a park and sitting on a bench became a common and enjoyable thing for Stephen and me to do when I was able to get out of the dorms. On this particular night, we drove on my favorite road several times. This specific road wound through the country and under a bridge. It was very peaceful. Some days we would drive for hours just to talk, sit quietly, listen to some new songs, or just be together. Many times we would have conversations about God and would pray together toward the closing of our time. I truly can't remember a time with Stephen that we wouldn't at some point find time to pray together. What a blessing it was to have such a man as my friend, my encourager, and my boyfriend.

As Stephen and I drove that night, he began to share something that was on his heart. He was very bothered about this particular thing. Very rarely did I see Stephen upset, and honestly most people thought he never got upset. However, he was still human and struggled with temptations. On the days when he would become frustrated, he would look at me and say, "Babe, please pray for me." That night he shared what was on his heart and his frustrations about my being sick. As we pulled back into the dorm parking lot, he asked if I would pray for him. Anytime Stephen asked me to pray for him, I always felt so honored and privileged to pray for my boyfriend. We parked and bowed our heads. I prayed for Stephen, my sickness, our relationship, our friends, and our families. Stephen joined me in praying out loud. We finished praying and Stephen walked me to the elevator like a gentleman. As I got to my room, my phone rang. Stephen was calling. He told me he was still stressed and was going to play basketball with the guys in the gym. Stephen still had a lot on his heart, but he simply said, "I love you, Katie, thank you for praying for me and blessing me in our relationship." I told him I loved him too and was thankful that our God had brought us together. I also told him to be careful playing basketball because I knew he sometimes had trouble with his heart during physical activity. But he always said it was nothing too bad. He told me he loved me again, and he would talk to me soon. I didn't know this would be the last conversation I would have with him on earth.

An hour and a half later, my friend Alyssa found me and handed me her cell phone. Stephen's friend Troy was on the phone. He had called my phone, but I had not answered. I was baking muffins in the girls' dorm kitchen, and I didn't have my phone with me. He told me that Stephen had fallen in the gym, and I should start praying. Troy sounded very shaken. At that time, I did not understand the seriousness of Stephen's condition. I was in shock, but I did not think that Stephen was in serious trouble. So I prayed for God's protection around Stephen but remained where I was. However, soon after I talked with Troy, my friend Bekah (the female Residence Director - RD) and Dean Cory, the Dean of our school, came rushing upstairs to find me. That was when a sick feeling in the pit of my stomach told me something was very, very wrong. However, I wanted to remain strong until I knew what was happening. Alyssa, Bekah, Dean Cory, and I drove over to the gym together. All I saw was the back of Stephen's shoes being shut into the ambulance as we neared the gym. I began to pray in my heart, "Dear, Lord, let Stephen be okay."

I rode to the hospital with Jon G., the male RD, (Stephen was Jon's Assistant Residence Director in the dorms), Dean Cory, and Bekah. We followed the ambulance the whole way to the hospital. As we drove up the ramp to get off the interstate, I was overcome with this horrible feeling. "God," I prayed, "if Stephen is going to die, take me instead. I'm already sick, so please, God, let him live." Then I began to cry. I knew God had everything in His control, but I was struck by the gut-wrenching realization that Stephen might be going home to Heaven. I didn't want to believe it. I would only believe it if the doctors told us he was really gone. So I put my hope on the thought he may still be alive.

I remember waiting in the emergency room. Dean Cory asked me if I was okay. I didn't know what to say. There was no information about what was happening. I had no certainty Stephen was going to walk out of the ER with his big smile warming all of our worried faces. All I wanted was to know that Stephen was okay, but I told Dean Cory I was fine. Dean Cory looked at me with concern, but then went and sat down by Jon. Above all things, I wanted to hope for the best, but in my heart, I continued to have this horrible feeling in the pit of my stomach. Dean Cory, Jon, Bekah and I waited for what seemed like hours, but it was probably only 30 to 60 minutes before a nurse came out and called for Stephen Reynolds' family. The four of us stood. Dean Cory explained we were not Stephen's family, but we were all from the college he attended. The nurse took us into a back room, and we continued our wait there. After waiting for a while and still not being able to see Stephen, I knew something was wrong.

We asked a nurse. She told us they needed to contact Stephen's family, and his family needed to come to the hospital. My heart melted to tears inside me, but outwardly I continued to hope for the best. I continued to pray, "God, please help. I need you, but above all, your way is best." We gave them Stephen's parents' cell phone numbers and continued to wait. Eventually, the nurse took us back to the original ER waiting room so that we could wait for the Reynolds family.

During the wait for Stephen's parents to come to the ER, many Calvary faculty members stopped by or stayed with us in the ER. The president of our college, two deans, and a few professors came to stay for a bit as we waited to hear news about Stephen.

Finally, Mr. Reynolds, Mrs. Reynolds, and Aundra (Stephen's sister) walked into the ER. It was about two hours after the ambulance brought Stephen into the emergency room. I walked over and greeted them. The nurse called them into a back room, and I asked if I could go with them. They said I could, and the four of us went back and sat down. After a few minutes, a doctor and a nurse came into the room. As the doctor began to speak, I watched as the nurse walked to a table and grabbed a box of tissues. My heart sank. I listened as the doctor introduced himself and began to tell us the events of the night. I can't remember exactly everything word for word, but this is what I remember the best. He told us Stephen's heart had stopped and there were many attempts to revive him. His friends tried to resuscitate him when he first fell. When the ambulance arrived, the EMTs had tried hard for 20 minutes to get him to start breathing and to get his heart going, but it didn't work. Then, when they brought him to the ER, the hospital staff tried for 30 minutes to resuscitate him to no avail. Around 9:30 P.M. They pronounced Stephen dead. Stephen was gone. He was really gone. We all sat there in shock. The reality of the news started to sink in after a minute. Mr. Reynolds had to leave the room to get some air, so he went outside. I just sat still; no tears came. My heart hurt, and I was in painful shock. Mrs.

Reynolds and Aundra also sat in shock until Mrs. Reynolds asked to see Stephen's body. The nurse guided the three of us down a hallway until we were standing right outside the room that held Stephen's body. Mrs. Reynolds looked at Aundra and me saying we didn't have to go in if we didn't want to. We both looked at each other and shook our heads saying we did not want to go in and see his body. In my thinking, I was too scared to see Stephen's lifeless body right at that moment. As Mrs. Reynolds walked into the room, Aundra and I hugged each other and began crying.

When Mrs. Reynolds returned, the three of us hugged and returned to the waiting room area. All of the people waiting there had received no news about Stephen. When we arrived, one of my professors, Mrs. M., walked toward me. I walked to her and said, "Stephen's gone." She took me in her arms, and I cried until my sobbing subsided. Afterward, I was able to go sit with the others. Dean Bailey came into the waiting room and gave me a long hug. She had been at the school taking care of all the shocked Calvary students while Dean Cory was at the hospital. As Dean Bailey hugged me tight, I cried again. That night, I was glad to have three mother-like hugs from Mrs. Reynolds, Mrs. M., and Dean Bailey. When my own mom was so far away, these ladies I love and respect so dearly showed me love by giving me those mom hugs.

I remember calling my parents and telling them the news. It was around 11:00 P.M. when I told them Stephen had passed away. They cried with me over the phone about the sad news. They knew Stephen had intended to propose to me in just a few weeks. That made it even harder to hear of his death. My parents were very supportive in my grief. I asked them to come down as soon as possible, and they said they would. They arrived the next day.

Then I called my brother Jonathan. When I told him the news, he also was moved to tears. Jonathan had never met Stephen, but he was planning to meet him at my college graduation which was two weeks away. After crying and talking for a bit, I asked Jonathan to pray. We both cried through the prayer, but it was greatly needed. I am very blessed to have a godly brother. After I got off the phone, my good friend Carolyn arrived. She brought with her another friend Crystal and our friend Jonny. They were all shocked by the news of Stephen's death, and we all gave each other long hugs.

Before we left the ER, Mr. Reynolds made me promise to come over to their house the next day. I promised him that as soon as I woke up the next day I'd come over. I gave all the Reynolds hugs then went back to the dorms with Dean Bailey and Bekah. As we neared the dorms, I asked if I could see Stephen's two closest friends, Stephen Buller, who is called "Buller" by his friends, and Troy. Dean Bailey and Dean Cory said they could make it happen. As we walked into the dorm building, I couldn't look anyone in the eye as we walked to the end of the hallway. The deans opened an empty room for Troy, Stephen Buller me and the RDs, Bekah and Jon G. The deans joined us as we spent time talking together. I hugged Troy and Buller, and we all cried tears of sorrow over the loss of Stephen. We all talked for about an hour and shared funny memories about Stephen. Even the deans and Bekah and Jon told a few stories or just joined in the laughter. In the midst of all the tears and sorrow, I still knew God is good. The events of that night were hard for all of us in different ways, but our trust in God's goodness remained strong. Never once did I hear someone yell at God in anger; never once did I hear someone speak angrily about God's plan or His will. That night, we honored God by putting our trust in His goodness. I praise God for helping us do that!

We all parted ways with hugs and prayer. I went up to my room and found Carolyn there. My other close friend Jill Ann was at her home for the weekend in Illinois but, after hearing the news of Stephen's death, she was coming back early by catching a ride with my brother Jonathan. My brother Jonathan was attending seminary in Deerfield, IL. Dean Bailey and Bekah did not want me to be alone that night, so they asked Carolyn to stay with me.

It was a long, restless night. I did not sleep well. I remember crying and crying and then crying some more. I remember trying to fall asleep, but all that came were tears. Sometimes I drifted off to sleep, but then I would wake up with tears tumbling out of my eyes. I couldn't stop them. Carolyn just lay quietly on the other side of my bed. Sometimes I thought she was sleeping, and other times I thought I heard her crying. I am thankful she was there that night. I'm also thankful that Dean Bailey and Bekah didn't want me to be alone. Crying with someone is so much better then crying alone. The sorrow of losing someone you love deeply is one of the hardest things to experience in life. My prayer was simple that night. "Lord," I prayed silently in my heart, "Your plan is better than mine. Help my unbelief." Over and over again, I prayed that prayer as the tears streamed down my face. I really wanted Stephen to be alive, to laugh with him, to have one more Stephen hug, to marry him, and to live my life with him. All of those things, although good in and of themselves, were what I wanted for myself. This was one of the hardest, saddest things I ever had to walk through, but my faith in God meant more to me than my selfish happiness and wants in life. Although my grief and sorrow were understandable, my faith in God was not shaken. I wanted Stephen to be with me on earth, but I knew he was in Heaven. That knowledge comforted me. I was finally able to drift off to sleep and get a few hours of peaceful sleep knowing that, though I was sad, God was my ultimate comforter.

CHAPTER 10

2 Corinthians 1:3-5
Blessed be the God and Father of our Lord Jesus Christ,
the Father of mercies and God of all comfort, who
comforts us in all our affliction, so that we may be able
to comfort those who are in any affliction, with the
comfort with which we ourselves are comforted by God.
For as we share abundantly in Christ's sufferings, so
through Christ we share abundantly in comfort too.

THE DAY AFTER HIS DEATH

The next day, I woke up feeling like I had cried all night. Have you ever seen a child who has cried so hard their face is red, their clothes are damp, and the sobbing continues to come from within them even though the tears have stopped? When I woke up, my eyelids were swollen. My pillow was wet, and I felt sobs catching at the back of my throat. It seemed that nothing about that day could possibly be good. However, I remembered that there was one good thing. I knew my hope and faith were in God, and nothing could take away that assurance. It was a bright day filled with sunshine, but the light seemed to have vanished from the entire campus atmosphere. Everyone sought hugs from fellow students or Calvary staff. Even though it was Sunday, not very many people went to church. Calvary Bible College was grieving the loss of a friend, classmate, mentor, and student.

As I sat up in bed, I realized Carolyn was gone, and I was left alone. I was fine with that because I had not had a moment to myself since Dean Cory and Bekah came to get me, and we rushed to the ER less than 14 hours earlier. I took a shower. As the warm water ran over my face, the tears flooded out, and I could not control the sobbing. "God," I prayed out loud, "Your plan is better than mine. Help my unbelief because I do not understand. Comfort me today. Comfort all of us today. Help me, Lord. Amen." The tears continued to flow. Gradually they subsided, and I finished my shower. I got ready for the day; then I sat down on my bed. The next thing I remember is waking up and seeing Bekah sitting in my room. Suddenly my phone rang. My brother was calling and saying he was on his way to Kansas City, and he would be there that night. My friend Jill Ann who had gone home for the weekend also called later. She told me that she would hitch a ride with my brother and would be there that night as well. Jonathan had called me as he was leaving Chicago. He still had a three-hour drive to Jill's house in Illinois. They traveled together from there to Kansas City, Missouri.

A few hours later, Troy, Buller and I were on our way to the Reynolds' house. We arrived early that afternoon. Stephen's two older brothers, two nieces and nephew had arrived shortly before we did. Many other family members and friends of the Reynolds came over to their house throughout the day. It was a long, hard day, but it was good to be around people who could understand the hurt I was experiencing. These people loved Stephen and were mourning his loss too.

Soon after we arrived, I remember Mr. and Mrs. Reynolds telling me they believed God had great things in store for my life. They had watched me go through hardships but still keep my faith in God. Because of that, they believed that one day I might speak on Focus on the Family (a Christian radio program) or become a famous speaker about what God has done in my life. At the time, I didn't know how to respond to that idea. I wanted God to use this tragedy for good in some way, but I didn't know what kind of role I was going to play in His plan. I haven't spoken on Focus on the Family or become a famous speaker, but God did direct me to write this book to share my story and to tell of His goodness. If it hadn't been for the Reynolds' suggestion about telling my story to a large audience, I may never have thought about being willing to share it with a lot of people. I wouldn't have thought about writing this book. It is my prayer that it brings hope, help, and comfort to those who read it. That's you, dear reader.

The rest of the afternoon went by like a blur. We sat around, ate barbeque, and talked. I tried my best not to cry because I don't like to cry in front of a group of people I don't know very well. We shared stories and memories of Stephen. After a long afternoon, we returned to the campus. My brother, Jill, and my parents were arriving that evening and meeting us at Calvary.

On the ride back, it was quiet. I sat in the back seat and cried quietly. Buller and Troy sat rather quietly in the front seat. Overall, the whole day was tough. When we got back to the dorms, I saw that my brother and Jill had arrived. Jonathan walked toward me, and I rushed into his strong arms and cried as my big brother held me. We cried together. When the crying subsided, I think I remember making a silly joke about snot or something of that nature, and we both laughed. I thank God for giving me the ability to laugh even when things were so sad.

Jonathan and I talked a little bit about the day as we stood in the parking lot of the dormitory. As we talked, I saw my two closest friends, Jill and Carolyn. Those two wonderful gals had stood by my side through the good times in life, the hard times of my sickness, and now Stephen's sudden death. They were standing with Dean Bailey and other people outside the dorms. I waved, signaling them to come toward us, and they ran down the hill to the parking lot until the three of us girls were hugging and crying.

Soon there was a group of us gathered outside the dorms. One of Stephen's friends, Justin, went to get us some fried chicken. When he returned, Troy, Buller, Jonathan, Carolyn, Jill, and I gathered around buckets of fried chicken and ate. Grief had given all of us, especially Carolyn, Troy, Buller, and I small appetites earlier in the day, and we hadn't eaten much food.

My mom and dad arrived as we were eating. I got up and hugged them both long and hard as I cried new tears of sorrow and grief. My parents joined our group, and I remember my parents talking to the deans. At this point, I felt like I was in a daze from the events of the past 24 hours. My parents had booked lodging at a hotel for a few nights so that I could get off the campus. I packed a few things, and we drove to the hotel. By the time we got to the hotel, it was around nine o'clock in the evening, and we were exhausted. We all decided to go to bed. I remember trying to fall asleep, but every time I closed my eyes tears came. I lay there silently for about an hour. As I lay with my eyes open, I prayed for God to let me sleep so that I could just get through the night. I closed my eyes again, and more tears came. My mind began replaying the events of the previous night in the ER and the time I heard that Stephen had died. More and more tears began to flow, but I didn't want to cry. I didn't want to think about the sorrow of losing Stephen. I just wanted him back. I began to pray the simple prayer I had started the day before, "Lord, your way is better than mine. Help me to believe it."

I decided to get out of bed. I left our hotel room and wandered down the hallway to the lobby. The man working at the front desk was a friendly man. I still laugh when I think about him. He was probably in his forties and talked to everyone like they were his best friend. Since I was in a state of shock and grief, I just wanted to be left alone. I walked into the breakfast area and poured myself a bowl of fruit loops. I walked back into the lobby and sat on the couch to watch something on the TV.

As I sat there, quietly eating my fruit loops and watching a cooking show, the friendly front desk attendant came out to chat. It must have been around two or three o'clock in the morning, so I could understand that he was probably bored. However, I was so emotional that it was a struggle to talk without crying. "Why are you awake at this time of day, Miss?" The hotel clerk asked me excitedly as if he was saying, "Hi," to his best friend. I looked at him and wondered if he could see I had been crying. I stared speechless at him because I did not have the heart to tell him to leave me alone, and part of me did not want to be left alone. Another part of me did not want to tell him the honest truth that, less than 48 hours earlier, my intended fiancé had died unexpectedly. Right now, I desperately wanted to be sleeping, but whenever I closed my eyes, all that came were tears. Finally I said, "I couldn't sleep." Then he asked, "What brings you to this hotel, young lady?" Thankfully he couldn't read my mind. I wanted to speak harshly to this nice man and tell him to leave me alone, but my kind heart couldn't do it. Hiding the tears I said, "My family came to visit me, and I decided to get away from my college's dorms." With that simple explanation, I prayed that the man wouldn't ask me any more personal questions. For the most part, he did not. He kept the questions and the conversation pretty light after that. Soon he left me alone to watch TV in silence. After about an hour, my mom came wandering sleepily down the hall. She had awakened to find me missing and was worried that I was crying somewhere all alone.

After my mom arrived, the clerk came back. The three of us watched the cooking show, but then that dreaded question came not from the hotel clerk but from my mom. It was the question I'd been trying to avoid with the hotel clerk. Mom asked, "Did you tell him about Stephen?" Tears began to flood, but I tried hard to fight them back. It was a fair question for my mom to ask, but she didn't know what I was feeling or thinking. I shook my head to say no. The hotel clerk seemed so friendly and interested, but he had no idea what he was about to hear. He asked my mom what she meant, so my mom explained a short version of why we were there. The clerk became sad, gave us his condolences, and soon after that left us alone. A wave of relief flooded over me as the clerk walked away. Mom and I watched the rest of the cooking show episode, sharing some small talk about the random foods they were making. The tears were finally gone, and I was beginning to become tired as the show ended. I told my mom I thought I could sleep, so we walked back to our room. I fell fast asleep as soon as my head hit the pillow.

THE WEEK BEFORE THE FUNERAL

The Reynolds planned Stephen's funeral for that coming Friday. As the rest of the week went by, I was still in a lot of shock. Every Monday night at Calvary, devotions were held on campus. This particular Monday, the deans arranged for an all-campus gathering for devotions. Normally, the girls and guys gather together, and the deans give a pep talk. Sometimes the male RD gives a devotional. On this night, it was a memorial service for Stephen. I remember the deans asking me what I thought would be best or what I would like. They wanted the service to be a time of worship, honoring God and remembering Stephen. I suggested they ask if Stephen's friends wanted to speak which I thought they would be willing to do. I told the deans about six guys who were really touched by Stephen's friendship and who I believed would be honored to speak at his memorial service. We sang many praise songs. Many of Stephen's friends talked about who Stephen was to them, their friendship with him, Stephen's love for me, and most of all Stephen's love for God. My brother also spoke which really meant a lot to me and Stephen's friends. I can't remember everything Jonathan said, but he talked about a passage of Scripture. He also mentioned the few times Stephen had called him on the phone to chat while we were dating. That night we laughed, cried, and gave out many hugs. We also had a time of praise and worship.

Although the gathering was to help the students with their grief, most of us walked away knowing that God's plan was better than anything we could imagine. We knew that He was going to bring good out of this tragedy.

On Tuesday, my family and I went to the Reynolds' house for the afternoon. It was the second time my parents and Stephen's parents had met. They had first met four months earlier, and we had all gone out for barbeque in Kansas City. I was saddened by the thought that they had to meet for the second time on such an occasion. It made me want to cry even more. I held back the tears as we sat in the Reynolds' living room and chatted.

Mr. and Mrs. Reynolds have such an amazing relationship with God. Although they were grieving the loss of their son, they held firmly to their faith in God and His goodness. Going through the grieving process with them was inspiring because their response to Stephen's death was so powerful. "We miss him. But he's with the Lord, and we can't wait to meet him there in Heaven!" Wow! They were saying this less than a week after Stephen's death. They continue to say it to this day. It has become a testimony they share with people everywhere. To this day, Mr. Reynolds will preach a sermon and gladly talk about Heaven. He'll say he's going to meet his Heavenly Father and see Stephen.

Stephen had many friends that he really poured his time and care into every week. As his girlfriend, I can honestly tell you I don't know how he made time for them all. Most people have a handful of friends with whom they are close and check in with every week. Stephen had between 15 and 20 guys that he kept up with every week. About two thirds were in the dorms, so that made it easier for him to invest his time into them. But the other one third lived off campus in different towns. Yet he still made time to call and talk with them on a regular basis. I know this because many times when we were on dates he would get a couple phone calls. Stephen would answer those calls if a friend needed prayer. Otherwise, he would simply return the call after our date.

Stephen's death came as a shock to everyone, and his friends received the news with a great amount of sadness. Because of his close friendships with all the guys, the news of his death was very hard on them. Troy and Buller contacted all the guys who were off campus and told them of Stephen's death. They asked them all to come to the funeral. Some of the guys arrived on Wednesday, and others arrived on Thursday. When I saw all of the guys that Stephen and I had been friends with for the past few years, it moved me to tears of joy. I had prayed they all could make it to the funeral, and they all did!

Thursday night was a reunion at Calvary. Some of our friends whom we hadn't seen for about a year came that night. Tears and hugs were all around the room. A gathering was created in the first floor lounge of the dorms for everyone who was close to Stephen. Girls from the Wolfpack and almost every single guy at Calvary with whom Stephen was close came. We packed about 30 to 40 people into that lounge. Ben and Buller two of Stephen's friends served communion to the group. They decided, since we were together, it would be most glorifying to God, not just to remember Stephen but to also remember Christ's suffering, death and the hope we have in eternal life with Him. After communion, we told stories about Stephen. As crying and laughter filled the room, I looked around and thanked God in my heart. "I know Stephen is in Heaven with you, and I'm still trying to understand your plan. But thank you, Lord, for taking care of me. I'm in a room full of people who loved Stephen and love me. They are my family, and I thank You for giving them to me in this hard time. I am blessed." As the night continued, people left to go to bed. I remained in the room. After a while, the only people left were Stephen's 15 close friends, my brother, and me. We all stood in a circle with our arms around each other and prayed for the funeral the next day. I gave them all hugs and told them that I loved them all. I also asked them all to sit together during the funeral if it was possible. Jonathan walked me to the elevator, and I went upstairs to my room where my friends Jill Ann and Carolyn were waiting for me. We all hugged and went to sleep.

THE FUNERAL

Mr. Reynolds had asked me earlier in the week to say a few words during the funeral service. All week long, the shock of Stephen's death would not let me think about what to say. I told Mr. Reynolds I would speak, but whenever I thought about what I wanted to say, all that came were tears. The words came to me on the morning of the funeral, so I wrote them down in a notebook in case I would be crying so hard that I lost my train of thought as I was speaking. Mrs. Reynolds told me the night before not to wear black. So I put on a green dress, Stephen's favorite color, and got ready for the funeral.

Calvary Bible College offered the Reynolds the use of the school's chapel for the viewing and funeral services. The Reynolds gratefully accepted the offer since the Reynolds church building is very small. The viewing was first. I walked to the chapel with my family, Carolyn, and Jill. As I walked to the casket and looked down at Stephen's lifeless body, I began to cry. Through the tears, I told my mom, "That doesn't look like Stephen. There's no life." I found all of Stephen's guy friends sitting in the chapel waiting for the funeral to begin and gave them all hugs.

Then my family and I were led to a room to wait with the Reynolds family for the funeral. I met so many of Stephen's relatives, but the main person I remember meeting was his Grandpa, Mrs. Reynolds' father. The reason I remember meeting him was because he was a preacher, and Stephen really respected him. I felt honored to meet someone whom Stephen admired so much. The funeral director lined us up, and we walked down the aisle into the chapel. I remember Nevaeh, Stephen's niece, holding my hand as I walked behind Anthony, Stephen's older brother.

The funeral was one of the most uplifting, emotional,

awesome, God-inspiring, and long funerals I've ever attended. I don't remember everything, but this is what I do remember. Neveah, Stephen's niece, who was about seven years old, sat on my lap. For the first 20 minutes of the service, she quietly patted her eyes with a Kleenex as she cried tears of sorrow for her Uncle Steve. Oh, how I hugged her tight and held her hand as she cried. We both missed Stephen so much. I remember Mr. Reynolds giving the eulogy, but I don't remember anything he said because of my state of shock.

When it was my turn to speak, I explained that I was Stephen's girlfriend. I talked about the godly example Stephen was to many people in his life. I talked about the Wolfpack and asked all the Wolfpack guys to stand. There were several other guys that Stephen had impacted that also stood. There were about 20-30 guys standing to indicate that Stephen had impacted their lives. The room held about 500 people. In a room that size, the twenty to thirty men who stood showed the huge impact Stephen had made on so many lives. I wanted people to see the positive role model Stephen was to so many individuals. I wanted them to see how Stephen made loving others a top priority in his life and the impact it had made on them. I told people that God is good no matter what happens in life. His plans are always better than ours. I was not able to cry even though I wanted to cry. I remember holding Moriah, Nevaeh's sister, and Nevaeh during different parts of the service and singing one of Stephen's favorite songs, "This is my Father's World."

After the service, we went to the gravesite. My family, Troy and Buller were in one car while Jill, Carolyn, and Buller's mom and sister were in another car. The Reynolds families were in their cars, and we all followed the hearse to the cemetery. It was a cold, dreary day. Not many people came to the cemetery, and those of us who were there crowded into the tent and huddled together for warmth. There was a small service at the cemetery. Afterwards, I gave all the Reynolds hugs, and my family took me back to Calvary.

I was not feeling well that day as far as my health. The whole week had been exhausting, and I needed rest. The Reynolds invited us to join them for lunch at the church and spend more time with the family, but they understood when I told them I was not feeling well. We went back to the dorms, and I took a nap. After a few hours, I awoke to text messages from some friends who had graduated from Calvary the year before and had come to the funeral to support me. I went downstairs to the lobby to spend time with them. I was thankful to have such good friends who came just to "be" my friends. A special blessing that night was having my friend Allison drive three hours to spend the evening with me by talking, listening, and caring. Throughout the days surrounding the funeral, friends sent texts and cards to remind me I was cared for, loved, and not alone.

CHAPTER 11

Ephesians 3:20-21
Now to him who is able to do far more abundantly than
all that we ask or think, according to the power at work
within us, to him be glory in the church and in Christ Jesus
throughout all generations, forever and ever. Amen.

GRADUATION

On May 9, 2013, the graduation anthem was loud and strong. All of us graduates donned our gowns and caps with tassels colored according to each person's degree. We listened to the graduation ceremony, received our diplomas, and smiled happily for our family and friends. It was a happy occasion. I was so grateful to be able to graduate despite my crippling sickness and Stephen's death. It was a lot to overcome while going to school! I was thankful to have my family, the Reynolds family, and my friends there to celebrate with me.

I graduated with an Interdisciplinary Studies degree in Biblical Counseling and Advanced Biblical Studies. I made it through the ceremony with few outward tears and took many happy pictures with my family, the Reynolds, and friends. I graduated alongside my good friends Jill Ann, Daniel, and Brandon. We were all proud of the diplomas in our hands. My family and I went out to eat with Jill Ann and her family, Carolyn, Buller, and one of our professors who had become our friend, Mr. Smith. Later that evening, I spent time with my friend Allison from my freshman year. She had come with her husband Nate and baby Titus. We spent time talking about life, and Allison taught me how to crochet! The day was filled with good memories. Again, I was blessed by God to have so many loving people around me and supporting me.

However, in the midst of the happy occasion of graduation, I was torn. It was supposed to be a grand, marvelous celebration for me, but grief remained with me. Throughout the ceremony, I fought back the tears. I missed Stephen and wished he was there to celebrate with me. All day, I held back the tears begging to flow from my grief of missing Stephen. Although my heart was sad, I did not let that stop me from celebrating with my family and friends that day.

After graduation I had to decide what I was going to do next in life. The original plan for me before Stephen died was to get an apartment with my friends Jill Ann and Alyssa for four months. Then in September, Stephen and I had planned to get married. When Stephen died, I was so broken I did not know what to do. I knew I needed to figure out something. I prayed and thought long and hard about the best option for me. I was still very sick, and the doctors in Kansas City were still trying to figure out what was wrong with my health. After Stephen died, I did not want to leave my friends and the Reynolds family. My two options were to go home to South Dakota so that my parents could take care of me or to stay in Kansas City. After a lot of thinking and praying, I decided to stay in Kansas City. I wanted to allow myself the freedom to properly grieve Stephen's death and to be near those who had been close to him. Also, I wanted to be close to the good doctors who would hopefully find out why I was sick.

After graduation, I rented a duplex with Jill Ann and Alyssa which was situated one-half mile away from a lake. In August, another friend and classmate, Sarah, moved into the duplex with us for the year. My roommates were huge blessings, and they all helped me throughout that year. God prepared my heart for blessings and healing over the next year. One of His biggest ways of healing my hurting heart was by letting me live so close to a lake. Because I was so sick, I did not work that year. I spent many days healing, both spiritually and physically, by walking to the lake and sitting on one of the fishing docks, pouring my heart out to God. I would sit in quiet solitude just listening to God's voice as He comforted me in my pain. I found joy in His creation, comfort in the wildlife of the lake, and blessings that made me smile every time I went to the lake. That year God brought a lot of healing to my broken heart.

One day as I sat in the solitude of the lake, I felt the Lord telling me to write my story. I felt this gentle prod from the Lord. "Tell your story, Katie." I didn't actually hear an audible voice saying that. I just felt the Lord leading me and putting a passion within me to write what was on my heart. So I started writing. As I began to write stories about what Stephen and I had experienced, it slowly became this book. I believe the Lord wanted me to write about how gracious He was to me and how He was my comfort and strength through such hard times. So the year after I graduated from college was spent trying to figure out my health, grieving over Stephen, and writing this book.

MY RING

A huge blessing came in the middle of that summer. I visited the Reynolds for a weekend. Earlier that summer, I had spent six weeks making a scrapbook filled with memories of Stephen and me. Dean Bailey, the women's dean, had suggested I make it. I loved the idea! It was a very healing and helpful process for me making the scrapbook. I put in all the pictures I had of us together, all the notes I had saved, and any other things that reminded me of our times together. When I spent the weekend with the Reynolds, I showed them my scrapbook and shared all the memories related to the items in the book. When I got to the end of the book, Mr. Reynolds told me there was one thing missing. I waited as Mrs. Reynolds went into another room and came back with a Jared's jewelry bag. My heart began to race. Inside the bag was a jewelry box. With my heart pounding, I opened the box. There, beautiful, precious and shining, was my engagement ring. It was the ring Stephen had bought but never had a chance to give me. It was a simple silver band with a small diamond. I like simple jewelry, and Stephen somehow knew that. I never found out if he asked for help or if he picked it out himself.

I took the ring out, held it in both hands, and then placed it back in the box not knowing what to do with it. After a minute, I took it out again, put it on my ring finger and said, "What am I supposed to do with it now?" With those words, I started to cry. Mr. Reynolds, Mrs. Reynolds, and Aundra all surrounded and hugged me. We all missed Stephen. Grieving wasn't easy for any of us, but it was a lot easier grieving together. Mr. Reynolds suggested, "You can put the ring in the back of your book." Mrs. Reynolds said, "Honey, you can wear that ring for as long as you want to, and then you can take it off." I appreciated both answers.

It was a couple of months before I wanted to wear my ring. For a few months I was grieving the loss of the dream the ring was supposed to have meant. After that time of grieving, I wore the ring for a year on my ring finger. Later I slipped a chain through the ring and wear it as a necklace occasionally to this day.

Many people close to Stephen knew he had purchased the ring, but they had no clue where he had put it for safekeeping. On the day of Stephen's funeral, I learned he had bought me a ring. Mrs. Reynolds asked Troy and Buller to find it so that I could wear it to the funeral. They never found it. In their despair on the morning of the funeral, Troy and Buller sadly told me that they could not find it and that Mrs. Reynolds really wanted me to wear it if they had found it. Mrs. Reynolds found my ring in Stephen's suitcase a few weeks before I visited them, two months after the funeral. The ring box was hidden by a dirty sock inside the suitcase!

That night, as I slept in Stephen's room, I cried tears of joy. I was blessed to be wearing the ring Stephen had intended to give me. I fell asleep that night saying, "Thank you, God. Thank you, God. Thank you, God, for your blessings and for taking care of me."

CHAPTER 12

James 5:13-16
Is anyone among you suffering? Let him pray. Is anyone cheerful? Let him sing praise. Is anyone among you sick? Let him call for the elders of the church, and let them pray over him, anointing him with oil in the name of the Lord. And the prayer of faith will save the one who is sick, and the Lord will raise him up. And if he has committed sins, he will be forgiven. Therefore, confess your sins to one another and pray for one another, that you may be healed. The prayer of a righteous person has great power as it is working.

MY SICKNESS

All throughout this book I've mentioned my sickness, but I never explained what it was or what I was experiencing. The truth is I didn't get answers until I went to Mayo Clinic in 2015. Mayo Clinic diagnosed me with fibromyalgia, chronic migraines, and a weak immune system. I struggled with many difficult symptoms during the worst part of my sickness. I will try not to bore you with extreme details. Here is a list, month to month, of the health problems I faced, the doctors I visited, and the answers I received from 2012 to 2014. It will help you see some of what I was experiencing health wise. Some of the answers and treatments helped. I also received a great amount of help from an allergist in

November 2012 (see chart below). But I really didn't get on a true path of answers and healing until I went to Mayo Clinic. For the years of 2012-2014, I was practically bedridden and needed help walking due to extreme dizziness. I relied heavily on my friends to help me accomplish normal, everyday tasks during this time. I am very thankful for all the friends that helped me.

DATES	DOCTOR VISITS AND SYMPTOMS
July 2012	• Went to ER the night I almost died • Diagnosed with a mold allergy • **Symptoms**: fatigue, headaches, concentration problems, excessive sleeping
August 2012	• **Symptoms**: Mostly stayed the same, but breathing improved
September 2012	• Went on gluten-free diet • Started to sleep even more (up to 20 hours per day)
October 2012	• Senses became heightened • Stopped driving
November 2012	• Went to a mold allergy specialist and received answers and guidance that helped
December 2012	• Started taking mold medicine • Started to sleep less (16 to 18 hours per day) • Started to breathe better and have less intense headaches • Senses started to return to normal levels • Dizzy nearly 24/7
January 2013	• Senses became heightened again, memory loss, head pain, weakened immune system • Trouble concentrating • Sometimes I would randomly fall asleep in class or just sitting somewhere
February 2013	• Changed general doctors

DATES	DOCTOR VISITS AND SYMPTOMS
March 2013	• Symptoms stayed the same as above
April 2013	• Went to a Neurologist • Got an MRI of my head and neck
May 2013	• Diagnosed with severe migraines. Migraines were almost constant. Migraine pain was an 8 to 9, with 1 as no pain and 10 as pain so severe you have to go to the ER • Started physical therapy twice a week. This was to help reduce migraines, gain energy back, and relieve dizziness when standing or walking
June 2013	• Went to a rheumatologist to see if there was something wrong with my muscles. Muscles were normal
July 2013	• Went to a sinus doctor. He found a polyp in my sinuses in the nervous system of my brain. • Went to a brain specialist to be tested for memory loss to see if my memory loss caused by trauma or actual health damage. The specialist said my memory loss was from trauma. When a person goes through intense traumatic experiences, they will have lapses in their memory. The body goes into survival mode. The things you knew before may be forgotten all together or slowly return over time. Sometimes people's memories heal for the most part. Other times people's memories become hidden for the rest of their lives. My trauma affected my long-term and short-term memory. I'm much better than I was, but there are days when I struggle remembering simple things. There are also some things from the past I just don't remember. • At the end of July I had my sinus surgery. I had eleven procedures done in about an hour!

DATES	DOCTOR VISITS AND SYMPTOMS
August 2013	• Had a CT scan to prepare me for sinus surgery. • During all this time my symptoms stayed the same, fatigue, memory loss, heightened senses, and migraines
September and October 2013	• Continued physical therapy to regain strength • After sinus surgery I started to have more energy and breathe better
November and December 2013	• Continued to heal, grieve and sleep a lot.
January 2014	• All Symptoms seemed to improve
February 2014	• Got my wisdom teeth removed
March 2014	• Finished physical therapy
April and May 2014	• My health continued to improve. Symptoms still plagued me, but not to the same extreme levels. Doctors said I was 65% percent better and had 35% left to gain back my health.

After reading that list, there may be some questions running through you mind. "How did I keep up with college classes?" "How did I have time for friends, homework, and dating Stephen?" The truth is it was HARD! However, as I keep saying, God is good. He is the only reason that I was able to do school, be with friends, date Stephen, and do the other daily things that needed to be done. He provided what I needed when I needed it. He worked it all out. For my senior year of college, I only had 12 credits to complete. When I got sick in July 2012, I thought I would have to move back home. That was when God provided the Surgeon family for me. I talked to the dean about my dilemma at the end of July because I was going to be an RA that coming school year. The dean suggested that I stay, be an RA and finish my few remaining credits, if I thought I could do it. I thought about it and decided to stay. I hoped I would feel better once classes started. I worked it out with my guidance counselors and the deans to divide my 12 credits into two semesters. With the dean's guidance, I also gave a little bit more responsibility to the Assistant Resident Assistant (ARA) on my hall.

I did six credits in the fall of 2012 and six credits in the spring of 2013. During the fall semester, I had two classes that met Tuesdays and Thursdays. That meant I only had to leave the dorms every Tuesday and Thursday, which was a tremendous help for me. The teachers knew I was sick and worked with me to finish well. For my 2013 spring semester, I had a three-credit night class that met once a week for six weeks. My last three credits was my senior project. My internship was supposed to have been my senior project, but I got sick that summer and couldn't complete my internship. My guidance counselor assigned me a 100-page paper discussing 50 questions about Theology and Counseling instead. The paper was basically a summary of what I had learned during my five years at Calvary about theology and counseling. This gave me the freedom to work on my senior project at my own pace.

That answers the question of how I kept up with my studies. Now I'll explain how I had time for friends, Stephen, and homework. I slept almost 15 to 20 hours per day. During my waking hours, I visited with the girls on my hall, attended classes, did homework, attended RA meetings, and went on dates with Stephen. I also spent time with Stephen and friends during homework times or meals in the cafeteria. Sometimes I would awaken after sleeping 12 hours and feel pretty well. I would call Stephen and tell him I was feeling well enough to go on a date or hang out with people. We would hang out with our friends or go to a restaurant alone for an hour. I usually didn't last very long when I was with a group of people. An hour or two was the extent of my energy level. Many times I would fall asleep while I was with friends. Everyone knew I was sick, so they would let me sleep for an hour and then wake me up. That hour of sleep would give me enough energy to finish homework and or enjoy some more time with people.

Everything I did exhausted my body. However, I did not let that stop me from enjoying life, but the longer I was sick the harder it became for me to be around people and to enjoy life. My head hurt all the time, and migraines ruled my life. Sometimes even a whisper felt like someone was screaming at me. I chose not to drive and relied on Stephen and my friends to drive me wherever I needed to go. Starting in December 2012, I was dizzy nearly 24/7 which made walking difficult. Stephen or my friends would walk me to class steadying me with their arm. It was a very tough time. Stephen, my friends, and classmates tried their best to help me when they could. God taught me a lot about patience and contentment that school year. He also taught me how to ask for and receive help from others.

VISION IN SURGERY

Grieving is a hard process to walk through, and summer 2013 was difficult. I was still processing the shock of Stephen's death and dealing with health issues, but I was surrounded by people who loved me. I also felt God's comfort and love deep in my heart. I found many blessings that summer despite the reality of grief. There were many blessings and a great amount of physical, emotional, and spiritual healing during that summer.

Sometime in the middle of May, I went to see the neurologist. She was very caring and helpful. She said I should go to physical therapy twice a week for the entire summer. This was to help me regain strength and lessen my migraines and vertigo spells.

She also wanted me to see an ENT (ear, nose and throat) doctor. Earlier in April, I had a CT scan of my brain and neck. A polyp was discovered in my sinuses along the nervous system of my brain. I went to the sinus doctor, and he scheduled sinus surgery for the end of July. He explained that there were also other things wrong with my sinuses, so the surgery would be about an hour long. He promised I would feel much better afterward.

My parents came down from South Dakota so that they could take care of me after the surgery. At the time, my roommates and I were still living in the three-bedroom duplex by the lake, and we had an air-conditioned garage. Whenever company came to stay, we gave them the only empty space available, the garage. Some of you may think we were crazy, but it actually wasn't too bad. We had two couches and some pictures in the garage to make it feel more room-like. My loving parents stayed in the garage for about a week while I healed from my surgery.

A week before I went in for surgery, a nurse called and told me to stop taking all of my medications. She said this would help with the anesthesia when I went into surgery. However, there was miscommunication at the hospital. The nurse did not realize that I should keep taking my migraine medication, so I stopped taking all my medications for a week.

The day of surgery came. It was early in the morning when we arrived at the hospital. Mom and Dad seemed as chipper as ever. The nurses were very kind and friendly. I changed into one of those very uncomfortable hospital gowns and waited as a nurse prepped me with an IV. My parents came into the room to wait with me before I went into surgery. Eventually the doctor came in and explained the process of the surgery. I was wheeled into a sterile room with several nurses and bright lights. The anesthesiologist gave me a shot. The anesthesia started to work, and I fell asleep.

What came next, well, that was a wonderful and awesome surprise! I remember opening my eyes and seeing Stephen. Yes! That's right. I saw Stephen Reynolds, the man I loved, the man who left this earth to be with his Heavenly Father. Standing next to Stephen in that vision was Jesus Christ! Oh, the great wonder and joy that filled my heart! In my vision, I was lying in a hospital bed in a recovery room. Stephen was on my right side, and Jesus was on my left side. I can't explain what Jesus looked like. The glory of light surrounded him. It was amazing just to be near Jesus. I felt as if I spent hours with them just smiling and looking at them, studying them to make sure they were really there in the room with me. I remember Stephen holding my right hand, squeezing it tightly and saying, "Keep pressing on for the Kingdom, Baby. I love you." He didn't actually say those words, but as we made eye contact, it was as if I could read in his mind what I needed to know. Stephen's smile was so big as I stared at him. Jesus was holding my left hand with such great strength and love. He said, "I know things have been hard, but I'll never give up on you. I have so much more for you to do. I love you, daughter. I will always take care of you." It was beyond wonderful. It was an experience beyond proper explanation. I can't put into words how deeply loved I felt. I had endured so many hard things, but this vision was a gift of love from my Heavenly Father reminding me how much He cares about me. I've felt so much peace since this vision. I know that, despite the trials that come my way, I'll be okay. I know I can survive any trial with Jesus by my side until my time on earth is finished. Whatever comes my way, I know God has a plan. I'm loved deeply by Him, and I'm a part of His perfect plan.

I remember lying in the hospital bed laughing with them when all of the sudden they disappeared. "How are you feeling? Katie, can you hear me? I think she's coming to." Those were the first words I remember hearing the nurse say as I came out of the anesthesia. I was so delirious from pain and anesthesia that I was confused about where I was. My head was pounding so hard. The nurse gave me four times the amount of pain medicine than the normal dose. Eventually, the nurse called in the doctor. Soon they realized that if I had been taking my migraine medicine the pain would not have been so severe.

The realness of my vision with Stephen and Jesus was so

emotionally difficult for me that I started to cry. I think the nurse thought I was crying from pain. She did not know that I had just had the most wonderful experience during my surgery, just hanging out with Jesus and Stephen. The vision had been so wonderful that I wanted to go back. I don't know where I was when I was with Jesus and Stephen. It wasn't Heaven, and it wasn't earth. But it was so peaceful and so calming that I just wanted to go back. Jesus and Stephen felt so real in my vision. I wanted them to hold my hands again. I wanted to be with them again. I wanted to laugh with them. My tears were from both joy and sorrow. I cried with joy because of the joy the vision gave me, but I cried with sorrow because the vision was over. I wanted to go back to that wonderful place, but I couldn't. My heart broke with disappointment, and I cried. As I cried, I realized the true meaning in what they had said to me. I was loved. God wasn't finished with me yet. God would keep providing for me as He already had been doing.

I felt like I was in a daze and fell asleep again. Everything started to make sense when I woke up the second time. It took a total of two hours for me to fully come out of the anesthesia, and I could leave the hospital. My parents drove me back to my house, and I spent the next six days in a recliner. My parents stayed for several days to take care of me before moving out of the garage and staying with friends who were 30 minutes away. When I was awake, my roommates talked to me. However they didn't expect their gauze-faced friend to really hold a conversation. There was also some innocent teasing about my appearance. I know I looked pretty terrible. Many good friends came by during that time to bring flowers or get-well presents. I was very blessed to have them nearby to support me.

On Wednesday night around 8:00 P.M., seven days after surgery, my nose started to bleed uncontrollably. After trying unsuccessfully for two hours to stop the bleeding, I called the on-call doctor, and he told me to go to the ER. My roommate Alyssa kindly drove me to the ER since my parents were no longer staying in the garage. I waited in the ER for six hours. I felt like I was in a daze.

Eventually, because I had lost so much blood, my weak body went into shock for a while. When my body finally came out of shock, I fell asleep in the ER. I again experienced the vision of Jesus and Stephen holding my hands in a hospital-like room. It was not as vivid this time, and they didn't say anything to me. This time, when I woke up, I did not cry. I felt even more peace after seeing them for a second time. The ER doctor finally put an absorbent plug in my nose around 4:00 A.M. I was so grateful to have my nose stop bleeding that I thought, *Praise the Lord!*

Alyssa and I left the ER around 5:00 A.M. My nose continued to bleed slowly through the plug. I was able to take care of my nose until I saw my sinus doctor. I waited 48 hours until I saw my sinus doctor on Friday morning. He cauterized my nose and told me what to do if it started bleeding again. Thankfully it didn't bleed that badly again. God was taking care of me.

I still think about that first vision I had in surgery. The peace from that vision still touches my life. Some days I just want the vision to return so I can be with Jesus and Stephen again. I know that God used that vision to strengthen my faith in Him. If it hadn't been for that vision, the recurrence of that vision in the ER, and the vision about having five minutes to live, God would not feel as real to me as He does now. When mountains appear in my life, I know without question that God is with me, and I know I can overcome them.

God is so good! Do you believe that? Do you believe He is taking care of you? So often I am filled with awe thinking about what God has shown me about who He is. The Bible says, "Delight yourself in the Lord, and he will give you the desires of your heart." (Psalm 37:4-7) I'm slowly beginning to understand what that means. I have to abandon all my selfish desires and humbly pray, "All I want is you, Jesus." When following Jesus and His plans for my life are the ultimate desires in my heart, it means my desires have become God's desires. Those are the desires He fulfills in my life as I delight myself in Him. There are days when my heart and my life fall short of who God wants me to be, but I continue to strive after God and His Kingdom. I end this chapter awed by God and what He has taught me. I can honestly say with all my heart, "All glory and honor and praise go to my Lord, the maker of Heaven and earth."

CHAPTER 13

Numbers 6:24-26
The Lord bless you and keep you; the Lord make his
face to shine upon you and be gracious to you; the Lord
lift up his countenance upon you and give you peace.

RAINDROPS AND RAINBOWS

I believe God is always taking care of us. As God's daughter, I know He has always held me closely from the time I first got sick, when Stephen died, and now at this point in life. God is just amazing! God cares about and grieves with His children. On the night Stephen died, it rained. The day we buried Stephen was a cold, dreary, and rainy day. On the one-month anniversary of Stephen's death, I went to visit his grave, and it rained on and off the whole day. Two months after Stephen's death, it rained. However, the day three months after Stephen passed away was a bright, sunny day.

I want to explain what was going through my mind on those days. The rain made me feel like God was crying with me. The raindrops felt like God's tears. It comforted me to know that God was sharing my sorrow with me. In the midst of the tears as the rain poured down, I remembered, *I am a daughter of God. He cares for me. I am loved.*

The sunshine on the day three months after Stephen's death

brought a new realization. I realized that I could still grieve, but I should not forget that my joy comes from God, not people or circumstances. Just as a rainbow follows the rain, so joy would follow my sorrow. I knew God was taking care of me. Though I still felt like I was in the middle of the storm, I knew a rainbow would come. And it did. God was my strength for whatever I was facing. He always has been, since the beginning of my life. When I see a rainbow in the sky, it's my reminder that God is caring for me, loving me, and bringing joy into my life no matter what I face.

On the eleven-month anniversary of Stephen's death, thunderclouds came and went all day in Missouri. It made me feel that on this day God was still grieving with me. The rain stopped as soon as I arrived at the cemetery to visit Stephen's grave. I walked out and stood in front of his gravestone. I thought I would spend my time crying, but I did not. Instead, I felt God's love and comfort surround me. I stood there talking to Stephen and God, telling them about what was happening in my life. Even though it may sound strange to talk to a gravestone, it was very therapeutic, and I knew God was listening to my life's joys and sorrows. As I left I felt a renewed joy growing within me. I was still sad and grieving, but joy was beginning to fill my heart. God was answering my plea for healing for my broken heart.

After that time at Stephen's grave, joy continued to fill my heart as God used His Word, people, music, and nature to brighten my spirits. One month later, as the one-year anniversary of Stephen's death drew near, I thought I would be full of grief. However, I was amazed to find joy placed in my heart by my loving Father. Slowly, the raindrops were giving way to rainbows.

BLESSINGS IN THE MIDST OF GRIEF

During my last year of college, when I first moved into my dorm room, I used Duct tape to write the words "I AM BLESSED" in capital letters on my wall. At that time, I believed that just living life was a blessing. God has since shown me that life itself is not the only blessing He gives. There are so many little joys and little blessings that He brings my way every day. Somedays He surprises me with big blessings that remind me how vast His love is for me.

Although loss and grief can occur in a short amount of time, the effects they have on one's life last for a very long time, perhaps a lifetime. One has to persevere through grief and loss and look for God's blessings, or become devastated. There is no way to prepare for loss. Even if God would have told me in advance that I was going to be sick for a long time and that Stephen was going to die, the daily process of walking through those hardships would still have been trying. Dealing with grief and loss is a daily battle. It can't be experienced ahead of time. However, there are blessings in the midst of the grief.

I experienced two types of loss. I experienced the gradual loss of my health and the sudden loss of Stephen. Looking back now, I can see that both trials strengthened my faith in God and gave me the opportunity to touch other people's lives in ways I couldn't have otherwise done or imagined. But walking through those experiences was still heart wrenching. During the hardest times and darkest moments, I struggled to see God's goodness. I cried out to Him many times, sometimes questioning His ways, but in the end I realized that I am nothing without my God. God is the foundation of my life. Without Him I would fall apart. My losses have been hard, but I have come to see so many blessings through my grief.

During the first seven months after Stephen's death, shock impacted my entire life. I lived my life somewhat robotically. I brushed my teeth to keep them clean, took showers to clean myself, ate food to sustain myself, and washed my clothes because they were dirty. Sometimes when the opportunity arose to have fun or be with people, I would tell myself, "Now it's time to have fun." I knew it was good to do fun activities with friends, but many times I didn't feel like having fun or laughing. However, since I knew it was good for my soul, I would talk to myself and remind myself I needed to do it because laughing and having fun was healing for my soul.

For a while during this time, I had one doctor appointment per week. I also had two or three physical therapy appointments per week because the doctor told me it would help me regain my strength. I cried many times before doctor appointments because Stephen was not there to pray with me or drive me there. Yet, in the midst of all my heartbreak, I was continually surrounded and supported by my friends, the Reynolds, my family, and Stephen's 15 guy friends. My friends who did not live in the Kansas City area called or texted me regularly. I was truly blessed to have such faithful friends.

When Stephen died, there was an unspoken promise made to Stephen by his 15 guy friends to help take care of me until I was done grieving and my body was healthy. They took over Stephen's job of caring for me. I gained 15 close brothers in Christ the day Stephen died. During the summer, Stephen's friends would come by a few times a week to see how I was doing. They took great care in making sure I was doing okay. I talked with at least 10 of Stephen's 15 guy friends almost every week. They became more than just friends to me after Stephen's death. They truly became my brothers and cared for me. Because of the close relationship they had with Stephen, we became a close family after Stephen died. To this day, we all have a deep respect and love for each other. Some of them still contact me from time to time, usually around holidays, Stephen's birthday and Stephen's heavenly birthday.

In January 2014, I started grief counseling with a grief counselor. I walked into the office for my first day of counseling so broken and needing help. Although I had been trained during my college counseling classes how to respond to a grieving person and how a person should respond to their grief, it was very different living through it in my own life. Mrs. C. was very understanding. I shared my life, grief, tears, fears, and hopes with her. It was so helpful and encouraging talking to her and telling her anything and everything on my mind. Because she was not emotionally involved in my life like my family and friends, she responded calmly and helped me think through what I was feeling. My family and friends were tremendously loving and supportive, and I was so grateful to them. However, there were many things I just couldn't tell them. It was a tremendous blessing to be able share anything I wanted to share. I'm very thankful for the six months I went to Mrs. C. and her willingness to let God use her to help me in my life. Looking back, I wish I would have gone back to Mrs. C. four years after Stephen died. It was good to talk with her in the midst of the trauma, but it would have also been rewarding to go back to her a few years later. I was able to process things more clearly by year four of Stephen's death. I think it would have been a beneficial and rewarding experience to talk with her at that time as well.

I am continually and totally in awe of how God has blessed my life. God's grace has been an anchor throughout my entire story. Laura Story, a Christian singer, sings a beautiful song named "Blessings." I'll share the chorus with you.

"Because what if your blessings come through raindrops?
What if Your healing comes through tears?
What if a thousand sleepless nights are
what it takes to know You're near?
What if trials of this life are Your mercies in disguise?"

I had heard the song many times before, but when I listened to "Blessings" just a few months after Stephen died, I began to understand the words in a new way. Tears filled my eyes as I realized that God had brought many blessings into my life, but many of those blessings had come through hard times.

God taught me a lot through the trials I experienced. I learned the joy of counting my blessings during hard times. I learned patience in waiting upon God's strength, will, and timing. I learned to be understanding toward others who are hurting. Above all, I learned I could not have lived this life without faith in the one true God.

FIGHTING BITTERNESS

The last three months of those first seven months after Stephen's death were incredibly hard. I went to multiple doctors, spent many days alone, and became very discouraged. As I struggled to find hope, peace, and joy, I clung to the only One who could truly help me, Jesus Christ. I spent my days with Jesus. I spent hours upon hours walking or sitting in my room just praying about my grief, for my family, the Reynolds, my friends, and the guys who had become like brothers to me. The time I spent with God was awesome, but I felt very alone because I did not have much human interaction. Part of the reason I felt alone was because my poor health did not allow me to have sufficient physical energy for normal life. The other reason I felt alone was because Satan was distracting me from focusing on my Savior and His boundless love for me despite my circumstances. Satan was continually trying to make me focus on myself and how miserable I felt instead of focusing on my many blessings. By Thanksgiving, I had started to become bitter and discouraged. Hopelessness began to settle in my heart, and I did not know how to combat it. I asked the Lord for help, and He answered my prayer.

During Thanksgiving I talked with my brother Jonathan, and he shared his concern that I was becoming bitter toward God. Jonathan and I had a long, hard talk that day while he shared his heart. As I listened, I became aware of the bitterness that I had slowly allowed to take root in my heart. I was angry at God because other couples had each other, but Stephen had been taken away from me. It didn't seem fair. It took some time to deal with the realization of the bitterness I was harboring toward God.

When I went home again at Christmas for a month, I prayed

for healing and forgiveness from God Almighty for the bitterness I had toward Him. Repentance and transformation began in my life as I worked out my feelings with God. Once I began to heal from the bitterness, I was no longer hurt or upset with God when I saw couples or married people together. Shortly after Stephen died, it was very hard for me to watch my friends get engaged and married. Stephen and I didn't get to enjoy the "engagement era" with our friends. I felt left alone while I watched others happily get married. It didn't seem fair! It felt like I took three steps backwards in my life while everyone else moved ahead with their lives. But God helped heal those feelings of bitterness and change my heart. Eventually I was able to truly be happy for my friends who were dating or married, and I could enjoy being around them. I was finally able to accept God's plan for our relationship even though it was different than what I wanted. I found joy in accepting the fact that Stephen was in Heaven. When I got rid of my bitterness toward God, I experienced His peace. I also received from the Lord an even greater love for my friends who were married or in dating relationships. I was excited, happy, and even grateful for their relationships with each other.

The first of Stephen's and my friends to get married was Brandon and Gabby. They got married at the end of March 2014. The wedding was beautiful and Christ-centered. I couldn't help crying as I sat between my friends Carolyn and Nichole. I cried because I wished Stephen could have been there to celebrate with our friends. I also cried because I knew I would never have a wedding with Stephen. I don't normally cry a lot, so my tears did not last long. Carolyn and Nichole sweetly held me during part of the ceremony until I was done crying. That was such a beautiful blessing.

I would love to tell you that since my heart change I've been a perfect Christian responding correctly to God and others in all areas of my life. However, that would be a lie. Since my initial realization of my bitterness toward God, I have been angry with

God at other times. There have been times when I let bitterness for some of the ways my life has gone creep back into my heart. I have questioned His sovereignty. I have been frustrated, and at times I have blamed God for the effects of what He allowed in my life. The list could continue for quite some time. I hope you see that I am a sinner saved by God's grace alone and not a superhero who gets life right all the time.

Did you know it's okay to have all forms of feelings toward God? It is! He understands. He wants you to be honest with Him about what you feel toward Him. He knows anyway. He is God after all. However, staying angry and bitter and continuing to question God's plan will not bring healing. Be willing to let go of whatever it is you are holding onto and place it in God's hands. Seek God with an open heart. Ask Him to change your heart and perspective and bring healing to your broken heart. James 4:8 says, "Draw near to God, and He will draw near to you." In our hurt, it's easy to shove God away. But if we want to be healed, we must draw near to Him in faith and accept the healing He offers. (Hebrews 11:6)

CHAPTER 14

Psalm 61:1-3
Hear my cry, O God,
listen to my prayer;
from the end of the earth I call to you
when my heart is faint.
Lead me to the rock that is higher than I,
for you have been my refuge,
a strong tower against the enemy.

THE BASKETBALL TOURNAMENT

On April 26, 2014, the day before the one-year anniversary of Stephen's going home to Heaven, there was a special celebration in memory of Stephen. Stephen's friends and I decided the best way to celebrate Stephen's life was to have a basketball tournament with a worship service afterward. I know it may sound strange to hold a basketball tournament in memory of a man who died after playing basketball. However, the reality is that Stephen didn't die because of basketball. God called him home to Heaven when it was time for Stephen to go home. It was God's timing. We all understood that. We also knew how much Stephen loved basketball even though he had to play cautiously. We were honoring Stephen's life by doing something he really loved. Stephen's greatest passion in life was God. The worship service afterward reflected that part of Stephen's life, as well as our own lives.

With the help of many people, we put together a three-on-three basketball tournament at Calvary Bible College. The main person to put together the tournament was Jon, a good friend of both Stephen and me. A few weeks before the celebration, my friends Stephanie and Daniel helped me create some memorabilia to give to everyone who attended the celebration. We ordered green dog tags with the inscription, "In memory of Stephen Reynolds," on the front in black letters. On the back in black lettering was written, "God is STILL good, Numbers 6:24-26." We picked green because it was Stephen's favorite color. A year earlier, soon after Stephen's death, Daniel, who was the student body president, created T-shirts for every student and staff member. The front said, "God is good." The back said, "We love you Steve 1990-2013 1-1-six." The 1-1-six stood for Romans 1:16, which says, "For I am not ashamed of the gospel, for it is the power of God for salvation to everyone who believes, to the Jew first and also to the Greek." Because Stephen demonstrated this verse with his life, the student body found it fitting to put it on the memorial T-shirts. I created the dog tags because I wanted everyone to be encouraged and reminded of God's goodness and to remember Stephen on this one-year anniversary.

The tournament went very well! Many people came to play or watch. Stephen's friends played. Current Calvary students played, and even new students who never knew Stephen came to play. After the tournament we had a worship service led by our friends, Dustin, Ben, and Jeremiah. We gathered outside on picnic tables and sang worship songs. All the songs we sang were songs that Stephen loved. During the middle of the worship time, I stood up and said a few words. I reminded people that God was still good even though we missed Stephen. Several others stood up and shared more memories near the end of the worship service. A group of us remained to play games and go out to eat supper. It was nice to spend time with beloved friends. Even though it was a hard day with conflicting emotions of sorrow and joy for me, God gave me His comfort and wonderful friends to make the day special.

April 27, 2014, came on a Sunday. The Reynolds' church was packed with many of their friends. I also invited many of Stephen's friends and a few of my good friends to come to the Reynolds' church service. After the regular Sunday service, there was a memorial service and then a barbeque. Many of Stephen's friends and my friends came. It was a blessing for me and the Reynolds to see the building so packed! During both services, God was praised and honored and glorified.

Those of us who knew Stephen still miss him and grieve our loss, but we have HOPE and assurance that we will see Stephen again in Heaven. Our journey has been hard, and many tears have fallen. However, our faith has not been shaken because God is the firm foundation of our faith. He is the reason we can sing and have joy. We know that no matter what happens in life, we can always say, "God is good"!

THE JOY OF HEAVEN!

Three children stared at me waiting for a response. It was summer 2013, several months after Stephen's death. Stephen's nieces and nephew just asked me if I am still Uncle Steve's girlfriend. Their eyes stared into mine with intent and interest as their question hit the innermost part of my soul. I wanted to pull Neveah, Chris, and Moriah into my arms and tell them everything is going to be okay. But I know that the pain of losing Stephen is not simply going to go away. "Yes, I'm still Uncle Steve's girlfriend. Do you miss him?" I breathed it out as tears threatened my eyes and a sob soared within my chest. "Yes," they responded and hugged me tightly.

Fast forward a year later. I was playing with the kids in the backyard at the Reynolds' house. As we were playing on the swing set, they all started to talk with me about Stephen. "Katie, do you still miss Uncle Steve?" I looked at them all, and said quietly, "Yes, I do." Then one of them asked, "Do you still love Uncle Steve?" As tears started to build within my eyes, I responded, "Yes, I still love Uncle Steve." Although it had been a year since Stephen died, each of us was still dealing with the deep loss and hurt. I asked them, "Do you guys miss Uncle Steve?" They unanimously spoke, "Yes," in agreement. Suddenly, Neveah, the oldest of the three, spoke, "I can't wait to get to Heaven!" I looked up from swinging with Moriah and asked, "Why is that, Neveah?" "Because, Jesus is there and so is Uncle Steve. I'm going to go to Heaven one day!" She said it so passionately that I knew she was serious. Chris piped up and said, "I'm going to Heaven too. I'm going to see Uncle Steve." Moriah responded with somewhat the same chorus.

Heaven! Oh, what a day that will be when I walk with Jesus on the streets of HEAVEN! People do not talk that much about Heaven. For those of us whose loved ones believed in Jesus and have passed away, we know they are in Heaven. Yet, we who are left on earth don't really talk about the fact that they are in Heaven. Knowing that our loved one is in a place we cannot imagine how wonderful it is should bring us much comfort. They wouldn't wish to be back on earth. They have been given a beautiful gift. They are finally and truly home with Jesus. They have no more pain, sorrow, or hurt. They are in a perfect Heaven. In my case, my heart sings out, "STEPHEN REYNOLDS IS IN HEAVEN!" That is amazing! This beautiful reality should not make people feel uncomfortable. This is why I shared with you the story of my talk with Stephen's nieces and nephew.

Did you notice the excitement and joy they had thinking about Heaven? Going through the grieving process is hard for everyone. However looking forward to being reunited with our loved ones in Heaven and no longer enduring sorrow and pain is something that offers great comfort. Those of us who believe the truth of the Gospel will go to Heaven too, and we should look forward to it just like Neveah, Chris, and Moriah!

Stephen's growing up years

Stephen as a kid at Disney

Mr. Reynolds, Stephen, and Mrs. Reynolds
at Stephens 8th grade graduation

Stephen and I

The cake Stephen made to ask me to the banquet

Stephen and I at the Banquet

Christmas with our closest friends: Carolyn,
Me, Stephen, Buller, Jill, Troy

Carolyn, Jill and I

*Stephen's artistic drawing of how he saw me
struggling to find God's goodness*

Stephen's artistic drawing of how he saw me finding God's goodness

Stephen and I on a date

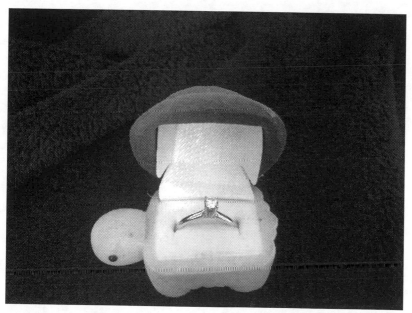

The engagement ring and turtle ring box

Some of the wolfpack guys and me a week after Stephen's funeral.
These guys were a blessing and support to me after Stephen's death.

Carolyn, Me, and Jill: These two were and still are faithful,
loving friends. I have been so blessed by their friendship.

PART 2

THINGS GOD TAUGHT ME THROUGH LOSS

I Peter 5: 10
And after you have suffered a little while, the God of all grace, who has called you to his eternal glory in Christ, will himself restore, confirm, strengthen, and establish you.

CHAPTER 15

A FIANCÉE'S LOSS

The tears have streamed down my face and my heart has broken in anguish missing the man whom I was going to marry. I was left to greet life's great adventures without my best friend by my side. There are books written to help wives grieving the death of their husbands, but there don't seem to be books for those who have lost the one they wanted to marry.

For those of us who have lost our fiancée or fiancé, it is a different, difficult road. Some are able to move on with their lives after a time of mourning. Others don't know what to do next in life. Honestly, my first reaction after Stephen died was, "I'm never going to get married." I know that sounds extreme, and not everyone responds that way. Yet my heart ached for the man to whom I had willingly given my heart. As time passed and God brought healing to my aching heart, my attitude changed. I learned to believe that if God did have someone else for me, He would soften my heart to be willing to experience that kind of love again. It took me awhile to be willing to befriend new guys let alone be willing to date. Through time and God's healing, I became willing to do both again.

If you have lost your spouse-to-be, you understand my loss. Our grief is difficult. We have a different journey than a widow or widower because we were not actually married. In preparing for marriage, we planned our future with our spouse-to-be. Our hopes and dreams were lost when our spouse-to-be died. The pain and sorrow are hard to accept, and the grieving process is different for each individual. It's hard to know how to move forward on your own without the one with whom you planned your future. I know that without God I would be a complete mess to this day. God has been my strength, my song, and constant comfort during my loss of Stephen, and He has shown me how to move forward with Him by my side. God will do the same for you. He will show you the way forward. He knows you are hurting, and He longs to bring you the comfort and guidance that you need. Ask Him to guide you, walk with you, and even carry you if needed. (Deuteronomy 1:31, Isaiah 40:11)

For those of you whose spouse or spouse-to-be is still here with you on this earth, God has given you a very special gift. Cherish that person. Thank God for the special person who sits beside you, encourages you, makes you smile, and enjoys spending time with you. Tell them and show them how much you love them and care about them. I'm so thankful that the last time Stephen and I talked we said, "I love you." Let your special person know they are so, so precious to you. You don't know if that one opportunity might be your last one.

"GOD IS GOOD" IN SONG VERSION

There are only three songs that I know of that are specifically titled "God is Good." These three songs have inspired, encouraged, and helped me through the many hard days. I would like to dedicate this chapter to the people who wrote these songs. Your lyrics and music are such a blessing to so many people. Thank you for allowing God to use you. These songs helped Stephen and me during such hard times.

Stephen and I strove to reflect and demonstrate the theme "God is good" with our lives. Inspiring songs were one of many things that meant a lot to both of us during my sickness. I remember the day when Stephen excitedly showed me the song "God is Good" by Christian rapper Da T.R.U.T.H. We both listened eagerly to the lyrics and played the song over and over again in the car as we drove to Red Lobster for a date. Tears ran down my face as we sat listening in awe. We understood what it truly means to have a good God. The chorus of Da T.R.U.T.H.'s song reads,

"They say life is hard, but God is good! We know God is good; yes He is good. We know God is good; yes He is good! We know life is hard, but God is good! They say life is hard, but God is good!"

This became the only song we listened to on many date nights. As Stephen and I heard the words, "Life is hard, but God is good," we would sing along knowing and believing the truth that God really is good and was taking care of us. I smile when I think of the days or nights we would go to a restaurant singing together, "Life is hard, but God is good."

Another song that ministered to our hearts was called "Because God is Good" by John Waller. The message of this song states the reality that God's plans are so much better than our own. It was a great reminder for Stephen and me when life did not go according to our plans that God's plans were better. In His goodness sometimes God cancels our plans because His plans are better for us. As a loving Father, He gives us better plans. The chorus states,

"When life doesn't go the way I thought it should Sometimes it's because God is good And when plans fall apart Though I never dreamed they would Sometimes it's because God is good."

The day we found this song, Stephen and I drove around Kansas City all day long listening to the CD. Never once stopping the CD, we listened to the words over and over, "When life doesn't go the way I thought it should, Sometimes it's because God is good." Stephen and I had a lovely time driving all over the city, and we had a deep talk too. We talked about our future. We talked about the possibility of my sickness never getting better. Stephen said, "Katie, God can heal you right now! We just got to have faith!" With tears in my eyes, I responded quietly, "I hope so." After a few minutes of silence I spoke, "Stephen, what if God doesn't want me to get better? What if it's His will for me to be like this?" Neither of us wanted that to be true. But it was on my heart, and I needed to say it. Stephen replied, "I don't know, Baby. I know God has a plan." We both wrestled with the answer, talking and even praying about it. It was a question we prayed about together for the rest of the time we had together on earth.

If God is a good God, shouldn't He heal me immediately? That was the nagging question in both our minds. A month after hearing the John Waller song, Stephen preached about God's goodness at the Calvary chapel in March 2013. He said sometimes we suffer, go through hard times, and experience pain. However, we can rest assured that our lives are directed by a good and loving Heavenly Father. I'm honored to have dated a man who was willing to accept God's plans for his life, even when they were not what Stephen had planned.

I was not able to share this last song with Stephen because it was written after Stephen died. Three months after Stephen's death, on July 4, my brother Jonathan came to visit. He said he had something to show me. When we were growing up, Jonathan spent a lot of time with music. He was passionate about playing the guitar and singing. He also wrote his own songs. This was one way we bonded throughout junior high and high school. He would write a new song and then sing it for me. I would listen and applaud and tell him what I thought of the song. When Jonathan said he had something to show me, he pulled out his guitar and a sheet of paper. He said he had written a song entitled, "God is Good." The song shows how Jonathan saw me at the time of Stephen's death and during the few months afterward.

"There are wounds, so much pain in my soul, they cling to me. So I bring them to the King, who binds them up so I can sing:

God is good. God is good. He's so good to me.
God is good. God is good. He's so good to me.

In these days I struggle on, to find my way, to sight my God. But I cling to simple truths, I hold them close; I cry to You.

You are good. You are good. You're so good to me.
You are good. You are good. You're so good to me.

God is working in the unseen for the
good of those He redeemed."

I felt so much love from Jonathan in his kindness in writing that song for me! I saw he was hurting along with me. He had great concern for my well-being. He saw that I truly did want to please God in my struggles. The lyrics and music beautifully described my life at that time. It was very special!

Each of these three special songs has helped me in so many ways. It is hard to even express it on paper. Music soothes the soul. It's incredibly hard to explain. Sometimes you just have to experience it. Songs have a powerful way of weaving together feelings and truth with a beautiful tune. God brought these three songs, all expressing the truth that God is truly good, at different stages in my life to help me through the losses I experienced. I continue to listen to these songs and sing along with them, saying over and over again that God is good. God has blessed me and has proven to be a faithful, caring, and comforting God to me. I am His child, and He is constantly by my side. I am never alone. How can I not sing, "God is good, God is good, He's so good to me!"

HELPFUL BOOKS

I want to share with you the books that ministered the most to my heart during the years 2012-2017. Those five years brought a lot of processing and healing. Maybe some of these books will be helpful to you for what you are experiencing in life.

The book that ministered to me the most of all was the Bible. The book within the Bible that I read the most was the book of Psalm. The Psalms ministered to my heart in a very deep and personal way. For an entire year, I read a psalm a day, crying out to God with the psalmist on the hard days and on the good days singing psalms of praise.

The book *Safe People*, by Dr. Henry Cloud and Dr. John Townsend, taught me a lot about trustworthy friendships. The book was very helpful in pointing out some truths about life. Some people in the world aren't trustworthy enough for you to share what's going on deep in your heart and mind. They aren't reliable when you really need someone to help you. They don't understand how to "be there" for you when you really need them. They aren't willing to walk through the hard times in life with you.

Other people don't know how to walk alongside you. They are not intentionally letting you down. Sometimes their life circumstances don't permit them to help out more, or they are not in a place in their own personal growth where they are able to help someone else. Sometimes, their personality will clash with someone else's, and they are not able to understand how to help a needy friend. Other times they simply don't know how to practically help a friend in need.

However, there are some trustworthy, "safe" people who can be trusted with precious information about your life. There are people who will walk with you during hard times and truly be there for you. Those people are priceless gifts from God. This book was very valuable to me as it helped me discern who in my life was "safe" and who wasn't. Distinguishing between the different people in my life helped me maintain appropriate relationships with them. It helped me stop holding everyone to the standard of a "safe" person.

My friend Carolyn saw the challenge it was for me to find joy during the hard days of being sick. One day she brought the book *Life without Limits* by Nick Vujicic into my room. The front of the book had a picture of the author. Nick has no arms or legs, but he was still smiling a gigantic smile. Carolyn left the book on my bed telling me she hoped it would bring encouragement and a new perspective on my sickness. As I read about Nick's life, I was amazed at his testimony. He was real, open, and honest. He talked about his hardships and the struggles of being born without arms or legs. As a kid, he just wanted to be like everyone else, but it was impossible. Nick finally realized that knowing Jesus was more important to him that fitting in with the rest of the world. When he finally came to that realization, his perspective on his physical situation changed. He never gave up his faith, and he accomplished many things people might say is impossible for a man without limbs. If you have never heard of him, I would encourage you to look him up on YouTube or get one of his books. He is a motivational speaker as well as an author. Through this book, I gained a new perspective on my sickness. The days were still hard, but I was encouraged realizing I wasn't alone in my struggles. Other people had different struggles than I did, but they still struggled too.

The Hiding Place by Corrie ten Boom tells the story of the ten Boom family during World War II. Corrie and her family hid Jews in their home during the Holocaust. Because of this act, she and her family were eventually imprisoned in a Nazi concentration camp. This book describes the hardships Corrie endured while she was imprisoned. My friend Jill Ann and I listened to a dramatized audio version of *The Hiding Place* by Focus on the Family on our way to an appointment I had with an allergist in Wisconsin. As I listened, I was reminded and humbled by another person who had gone through hardships and remained strong in her faith. Corrie never stopped praising God. Even when tortured for doing good, she continued to say, "God is good." As the audio book ended, my resolve for believing "God is still good" returned to my heart. I was not going to give up hope or my faith in my God.

Nancy Leigh DeMoss (now Wolgemuth), a gifted woman of the Lord, is an internationally-known Christian speaker and author. Her book *Choosing Gratitude* was given to me by my mom at the perfect time. I was becoming discouraged and losing my joy. My mom sent me this book and suggested I start counting my blessings. This happened around January 2013 which was the same time frame when Stephen sang "Count Your Blessings" to me. From that time on, Stephen encouraged me to make a habit of counting my blessings. It was a total God thing! Two people who were very close to me suggested that I needed to start counting my blessings. It is crazy awesome how God works! His timing is perfect. Counting my blessings was a huge step in emotional healing for me. As I read through the book, it challenged me to have a heart of gratitude instead of ingratitude. The book explained when I complained or grumbled I was being selfish. When I was grateful and thankful, I was giving thanks to God. God used this book to help transform and humble me. I learned to reevaluate my situation and thank God for what I *did* have instead of complaining about what I *didn't* have. During this time my mom also suggested I keep a praise journal and sent a journal with the book. As I read through *Choosing Gratitude* I started a praise journal. I have kept up with praise journaling to this day. I am terrible at doing just regular journaling every day, but something about a praise journal has been different for me. Almost every day since January 2013, I have found time to write praise and thanksgiving to God. I have finished over 20 praise journals. It has become a good habit and blessing for me in my relationship with God.

This next book meant a lot to me right after Stephen's death. Jeremy Camp, who is a well-known Christian musician, wrote an autobiography called I Still Believe. He wrote about how he discovered more of who God is and grew stronger in his relationship with Jesus Christ because of some hard life experiences. I listened to Jeremy Camp's music as I was growing up, but I did not know what he had gone through in his life. As I read through the book, I realized he had experienced something similar to what I had experienced when Stephen died. Jeremy's first wife died of cancer after only months of married life together. Jeremy wrote I Still Believe after Melissa died. I cried as I read through every chapter. My brother Jonathan gave me this book as a college graduation present. As I read the book one month after Stephen's death, I connected deeply to Jeremy's story. It was healing for me read to about someone who had gone through a loss similar to mine yet was still passionately living for God. This book still encourages me when I think about it.

Lament for a Son by Nicholas Wolterstorff is a book about grief and loss. It describes the grief Nicholas experienced when his son died in his twenties. My brother Jonathan sent me the book saying he didn't know if it would be helpful to me or not, but it was recommended to him by a friend. Although I was a fiancée and not a father, the book still offered helpful insights about grief and loss.

Randy Alcorn wrote a book called, 90 Days of God's Goodness. It is more like a 90-day devotional than a reading book. During Thanksgiving in 2013, my mom gave me this book. I was excited when I saw the title. To me the title seemed to say, 90 Days of GOD IS GOOD! This book offers insight into some reasons why we experience hardships as Christians and how we can respond to them. It also has testimonies from many people who have gone through hard times and are still striving to learn more about God even though they are still poor, needy, and sick. It encouraged me to keep following God, knowing that when I am weak He is there to pick me up!

Heaven by Randy Alcorn is an in-depth book about Heaven. My friend Mrs. M. introduced me to this book and encouraged me to add it to my library. It challenged my understanding about Heaven by encouraging me to use more imagination and to have a broader perspective about this glorious place. As I read about Heaven, I became more and more excited. I cannot wait to get to Heaven! I cannot wait to see my Savior and my God. What a glorious day it will be when I walk the streets of gold with my God!

About a year after Stephen's death, several friends and I read *Restless* by Jennie Allen. That book met me where I was at in life at that time. It describes longing for more of God and having dreams, passion, and purpose in life. However, it also addresses the fears and insecurities we have in life. I'm learning how to live my life again as a single person, how to face my fears and insecurities, and how to dream new dreams and live out my passion for God. God is my strength, my song, and ever-present help when I am in need. Although life is different than I hoped it would be, I'm willing to enjoy it. I'm willing to face my fears and sing at the top of my lungs, "God is good!"

I read C.S. Lewis's book *The Problem of Pain* in 2014 as I continued to seek God in my healing from grief. Lewis asks and answers the question, "How could there be a good God who allows His creation to suffer pain?" It is an in-depth book that makes you think. However, it is written in an understandable and relatable way. I would highly recommend this book to anyone going through any sort of loss.

I was talking with some college friends about loss and grief one fall day in 2014 when a friend suggested I read Gracia Burnham's book. I had heard of Gracia Burnham because she was a graduate of Calvary Bible College. Her youngest son had even been in my classes at Calvary. I knew she had written a book about her captivity in the Philippines, yet I had never had a chance to pick up her book and read it. But in that time of healing, I was willing to read her book. I went to Calvary's campus and bought her book *In the Presence of My Enemies*. It gripped my attention the whole way through. Gracia tells her story of being kidnapped with her husband Martin in the Philippines, losing her husband, and forgiving and ministering to her kidnappers. This book showed me a real-life example of loving and following God no matter what your loss may be.

My healing process continued in 2015 as I decided to pick up the book *Crazy Love* by Francis Chan at a Christian book store. I was hungry for even more of God and understanding His love. It explains God's radical love for all people, which was something I really needed to hear at that point.

Ann Voskamp has a beautiful way with words in her book *The Broken Way*. She is real and open, writing to those seeking God in their brokenness. She explains the vital importance of having our identity in God. She also discusses how our brokenness may seem to shatter us, but it can draw us closer to Jesus. She challenges us to love even when our hearts are breaking. I learned a lot about being bold in my brokenness because of this book.

Jennie Allen, a wonderful lady, wrote a book called *Nothing to Prove*. She writes about not giving up and trying hard to follow God no matter what our circumstances. I learned how to be satisfied in God without needing to prove to people who I am.

During the spring of 2016, my lady's Bible study at church read the book *Brokenness* by Nancy Leigh DeMoss (now Wolgemuth). Each person goes through brokenness in life. That brokenness can affect how we look at God and each other. I learned how God can continue to use my brokenness for his glory.

I read *When God Doesn't Fix It* by Laura Story in the fall of 2017. I found myself healing in many ways from my losses but still trying to overcome certain fears and insecurities because of my losses. Laura writes about the life lessons she learned when her husband was diagnosed with a brain tumor and what they went through. She explains that God may not fix everything how you want in life, but He can use your hardships to make you better.

Through all these books, I learned that I cannot change my broken, grief-stricken journey, but who I am because of that journey is my story of God's goodness.

CHAPTER 16

Philippians 4:11-13
Not that I am speaking of being in need, for I have
learned in whatever situation I am to be content. I know
how to be brought low, and I know how to abound. In
any and every circumstance, I have learned the secret
of facing plenty and hunger, abundance and need. I
can do all things through him who strengthens me.

ATTITUDE CHECK

At times, I had a bad attitude as I faced the trials in this book. I honestly thought at different times, "God, why would You let all this happen to me?" I grumbled and complained about wanting a healthy body again. Sometimes, I would wistfully wish that the man I loved would come back and visit me. (I never actually asked God to send Stephen back to earth because I knew he was in a much better place in Heaven.) That wish was unrealistic, I know. I was hurting, and I was asking for what I thought would relieve the pain. I wished for one last day and one last talk with Stephen. Every time I had those thoughts, I would be frustrated for a while as I focused on my hurt and pain.

Over time, the Holy Spirit gently refocused my mind on God and reminded me that my complaining attitude was not pleasing to God. God began to transform my heart, and my attitude gradually changed. My response then became, "God, being sick has drawn me so much closer to You, so I don't have to get better. I just want more of You. As for Stephen, I am so lonely, and I miss him so much. Fill my loneliness with more of You and bring friends and family into my life to help me not be lonely." My prayer was inspired by Psalm 73:25-28. I prayed this many times as the Holy Spirit continued to change my heart and attitude, and God answered those prayers. He surrounded me with people who loved me when I desperately needed them. He also filled me with more of Himself.

Overcoming trials, pain, hardships, and tears is very difficult. Have you ever sat in your car or in your room or taken a walk and complained to yourself? Maybe you complained to God? Let's see, the complaints might have looked something like this.

- *Life's not fair!*
- *My life stinks!*
- *Why does everything in my life keep going wrong?*
- *Who put all these bad things in my life?*
- *I just want to be happy!*
- *Why am I always sick?*
- *Why won't that one person just stay away from me? On top of all my hard trials, I have to deal with that annoying person!*
- *I'm never going to trust anyone again.*
- *I didn't do anything wrong, and things keep going wrong.*
- *Everything just went wrong today. I was late to everything. My boss got angry with me, and then when I got home there was NO food in the house!*
- *When will the tears stop?*
- *My car's broken...again.*
- *Will the pain ever stop?*
- *The bills are coming in faster than the income.*
- *Will I ever feel love again?*
- *Everyone else's life seems so much better than mine!*

- *Will I ever get well again?*
- *Life seems so overwhelming right now.*

What's running through your head?

Do any of those statements sound familiar for your life? They can be very real, true-to-life complaints. However, it's easy to have a bad attitude in the midst of trials. Instead of trying to work through the difficulties and find blessings in the hardships, it is easier to say, "Woe is ME!" It is easy to focus on ourselves and grumble when life is not going how we wanted.

Attitude is key! I was thinking about how easy it is to complain and pass the attitude onto others. Once I was surrounded by a group of people who were complaining. They had a reason to complain. But did that make it right for them to complain? I found myself wanting to grumble and complain with them. Their attitudes had been passed on to me.

It is often easier to grumble about the hard things in life than to rejoice in the good things in life. Why is this? Because if life is not going your way, then all you want to do is complain. The "Woe is ME" sign blinks in your mind every three seconds and makes it really hard to think about anything else. I encourage you to think about these verses when you are considering complaining.

> "Do all things without grumbling or disputing, that you may be blameless and innocent, children of God without blemish in the midst of a crooked and twisted generation, among whom you shine as lights in the world, holding fast to the word of life, so that in the day of Christ I may be proud that I did not run in vain or labor in vain." (Philippians 2:14-16)

It is a lot easier to complain than to be thankful when hard times are falling into your lap. You may not think you complain much. Maybe you don't. But stop and consider if you complain more than you give thanks.

Be intentional about being thankful. Look for ways to count your blessings. Change your attitude when you noticing yourself slipping into a habit of complaining. Ask God to change your heart and attitude so you can "shine like lights in the world."

As you have seen, throughout the events of my life I have overcome multiple obstacles. There are other obstacles that I am still overcoming. God is still a good God even in the hardships that we face. I will say this over and over again because I believe it. The things that have helped me the most to overcome trials in my life are the following:

- Reading my Bible
- Taking time to sit, process, pray, and just be still
- Writing down the thoughts running through my head to help me process what was happening in life
- Having good friends and family come alongside me, support me, and pray with me

I discovered that writing out my problems to God was helpful for overcoming an attitude of complaining. I would write down a complaint or a problem and pray about it. Then I would take that paper and throw it away, trusting that God knows best. I no longer had to dwell on the problem because I gave it to God. This doesn't mean I didn't complain anymore. I am human after all! I still complain sometimes. But I have discovered that complaining doesn't fix my problems, and it only makes the issue worse. Doing the above activities helped me stop complaining as much and find the blessings in the midst of the trials. What are some ideas you can do to help you lessen your complaining?

BE REAL

During our relationship, Stephen told me that, when he first met me, one of the things he found attractive in me was the fact that I was real. He said not many people in the world are real. Our definition of "being real" was being honest about what is happening in our hearts and lives. Sometimes it's easy to put on pretend smiles and try to make everyone believe we are okay. But that's not the reality of life all the time. Sometimes life is really wonderful, and our smiles are genuine. But other times, life is really hard, and we try to hide what is really happening.

Being real as humans, especially as Christians, is one of the most important things we can do. We need to be real about our lives. We love to share and tell people about the good times we go through, but we need to be real about the hard times too. It is vital to be real and honest about our pains, our trials, and even our grief. Yes, we need to be careful and discerning about with whom we are being vulnerable. We don't have to be vulnerable with everyone. We also need to be sensitive to the person who is listening. However, it is not wrong to be open and honest about the hard times in life. Be real with people. Begin with those whom you trust and start being open with them. Life can be hard, but God is good! Be real about it! I say this with love. I write this from my heart. The idea also comes from the sermon Stephen preached in February 2013, not long before he died. This comes from both our hearts. Be open and real with people and show the world how to be real in a Christ-like manner. Be real!

SUPPORTING EACH OTHER IN HARD TIMES

After Stephen died, I discovered that people treated me differently. They were incredibly cautious about what they said in conversations with me. They weren't sure if they could laugh around me. They weren't sure if they could cry around me. They weren't sure how I would respond to anything they said.

Grief is a hard thing to experience. I have discovered that most people who lose a loved one don't want people to start treating them differently. It's really hard to explain, but I'll do my best. When I was grieving, sometimes I wouldn't be invited to events that I would have normally been invited to attend. My friends didn't want to trigger a grieving moment for me. Also, when we did spend time together, they were really cautious when talking about death, dating or their personal struggles because they didn't want those topics to upset me. Even though grief is hard, grieving people still want to be told about events even if they decide not to attend. Otherwise, it feels like they are being forgotten. However, I do understand that it is really hard to find the balance for conversations and activities with someone who is deeply grieving. Sometimes asking the grieving person how they would like to be treated will help everyone involved. Open communication instead of quiet assumptions is often more helpful.

Although my friends and family were going through their own struggles, they felt like they couldn't discuss their problems around me. I'll give you an example. A friend would talk about how hard a class was and then apologize for sharing their hardship. They would then say something like this, "I'm sorry my life isn't as hard as yours." Although I know they said it out of kindness, my response to them was, "STOP! You cannot say that! No one can say that their life is better or worse than mine. Each person's life is different than another's life, so how can we even compare ourselves to each other?" I would say this so strongly it might have surprised some people. I did not intend to lecture others. I simply wanted them to stop treating me like my life was more difficult than their lives. I didn't realize at first how much it upset me for people to treat me this way. They wanted me to be real about my life and the grief I was experiencing, but they didn't want to be real about their lives. Somehow that reasoning felt one-sided to me.

I know they were just trying not to add to my emotional burden, but it ended up hurting me more than helping me. It seemed like they viewed me as unable to help them with their problems, but they were capable of helping me with my problems. Even before I met Stephen, I had always been real with people and wanted people to be real with me. I understand that it is important to be sensitive to those around you who are going through hard times. There are certain times when bringing up hard subjects will only add to their emotional stress. However, since everyone's life is so different, how can we really "compare hardships"?

I believe that instead of comparing our lives to each other we should come alongside each other in times of need. We should pray for each other during hard times and ask how we can help each other. What worked for one person isn't always what the next person needs. It's okay to tell a hurting friend you want to help them but have no idea how. Ask them what they would like from you. If you are the grieving person, don't assume that people are forgetting or ignoring you or even know how to help you or treat you. Sometimes they would really like to help, but they have no idea how to do so. Perhaps what they are currently trying to do isn't helping you. If you are able, communicate with them what would be helpful for you.

However, we must keep in mind that we often cannot "fix" each other's trials. God is the only One who can truly help us overcome hard times. Our hope and trust should be in Him more than other people. He is the ultimate Comforter and Helper. (Psalm 34:18)

My trials, pain, and tears are different from yours. You cannot compare your hard times with mine. I can't compare my hard times with yours. However, we can relate to each other in our hard times! We are never going to be exactly alike. God created us uniquely different. (Psalm 139:14) Therefore, our trials are going to be different, and our response to those trials is going to be different. For me, it was more of a blessing to have my friends walk alongside me during my trials than to have them tell me how much harder my life was than their lives.

CHAPTER 17

Psalm 34:17-19
*When the righteous cry for help, the Lord hears
and delivers them out of all their troubles.
The Lord is near to the brokenhearted
and saves the crushed in spirit.
Many are the afflictions of the righteous,
but the Lord delivers him out of them all.*

WHY I STILL BELIEVE GOD IS GOOD

At this point in my story, you might be asking some of the same questions many people asked me in person as I struggled through the hardships recorded in this book. Some people wondered if my sickness was caused by Satan attacking me, or a demon tormenting me. I believe those things happen, but I did not believe that was my story. I still don't believe my sickness was caused by a demon. Stephen was willing to try different options to help me get better. One time, he wanted to go to an evening service where they could possibly cast out the demon that might be causing my sickness. We were both desperate for me to be healed, but I felt uneasy about the service. In the end, we decided not to go.

I remember multiple conversations with Stephen when I asked him, "What if God doesn't heal my body?" Stephen would respond, "Don't give up hope. God can do miracles." I would then ask,

"But what if God can do greater things in my life through this sickness?" He would reply, "Maybe, Baby, but never give up hope that God can heal you. Never stop praying for healing, or you may doubt God's ability." It was wise counsel for me. I still think of his statement as there have been times I stopped praying for healing and doubted God's ability to heal me.

Then Stephen's death came. People felt sorry for me. They didn't know what to say when I told them my intended fiancé died. Many people would ask why I got sick, how Stephen died, and why these horrible things happened to me. I seemed like such a nice person. Why would God allow bad things to happen to me? I received multiple types of questions because of my unshaken faith. "Why would you continue to obey God and find hope and strength in Him?" "Why would you serve Someone Who allowed all these trials in your life?" "Why is God such a big deal to you?" "Why do you still believe God is so good?" "Have you done anything to deserve these trials?" (I could really relate to Job in the Bible in this area.) Dear reader, can you relate to this? It's a very hard place to be in life, isn't it? It's hard enough to wonder about these questions yourself. Having others ask you these questions and expect you to answer them is an even harder place to be. Yet, God was there with me, helping and encouraging me along the way.

When people asked how Stephen died, I explained the situation. I would often also talk about my firm belief in God's goodness despite my loss. My comments were often met with a look that said, "That's nice that you have faith, but I don't understand your faith." The same scenario happened with conversations about my poor health. That was one of the major reasons I wanted to write this book. I wanted to be able to explain my Christian faith and my belief in God's goodness in more detail than in just the short conversations I often had (and still have) with people.

My story must contain God's goodness. Without it, I would be hopeless. Because of my trust in God, I found so many blessings in the midst of my trials. I saw Him loving me and caring for me in the midst of my hurt and sorrow. I chose to focus on the good and not the bad. I chose to find hope in the midst of my hardships. Because of all I went through, God became an even bigger part of my life. My belief in God's goodness and my faith are what make my story beautiful. They are the foundation of my life.

This section is meant to show you from the Bible why I believe God is good. I believe God is good because I believe everything the Bible says is true. The Bible is the words God inspired men to write down for all people. Contained in the Bible are the reasons I haven't given up on my faith.

First, I want to start with an explanation of Who God is.

- God is three persons in one being. (Matthew 3:16-17) These verses show all three persons operating at the same time. God the Father was speaking from Heaven. Jesus, the Son, was being baptized on earth, and the Holy Spirit was descending on Jesus in a form like a dove. This is what people mean when they say, "Father, Son, and Holy Spirit." (Matthew 28:19) This concept is called the "Trinity." Jesus is the Son of God who came down from Heaven to earth to be born as a baby. When He became a man, He died on a cross for the sins of the entire world. After being in the grave for three days, He came back to life and returned to the Father in Heaven. God the Father is the Creator and Ruler of the world Who loves everything He created. (Genesis 1:1) The Holy Spirit lives inside those who have accepted Christ as their Savior to guide and comfort them. (John 14:16, 17)
- God is one in unity. All three persons are united in purpose. (Deuteronomy 6:4)

I realize that is a very short, simple explanation for a concept that is very difficult to understand. However, this book is not mean to be a theological book. It is meant to share my story and my faith.

I have listed other resources in the back of this book if you would like to learn more about Christianity.

If you have ever gone to Sunday school, it is very likely you heard the verse Genesis 1:1, "In the beginning, God created the heavens and the earth." It is the first verse in the Bible, and it explains Who God is. He is the Creator of all things. God is infinite and unchangeable. He is holy and good. He is all-knowing and just. He always has been and always will be. He is God. "Before the mountains were brought forth, or ever you had formed the earth and the world, from everlasting to everlasting you are God." (Psalm 90:2).

When God created the world, He created humans in His own image. Genesis 1:27 says, "So God created man in his own image, in the image of God he created him; male and female he created them." The names of His first human beings were Adam and Eve. All humans were made to reflect the beautiful image of our Creator God. Because I am created to reflect the image of the Creator of the universe, I know my life has value, worth and significance. That is true for all humans. Therefore, every human life has value, worth, and significance.

At the beginning of the world, God put Adam and Eve into a beautiful garden. This gorgeous Garden of Eden was in a perfect world. There was no death, suffering, or evil. It was perfect. In the garden were two special trees, the tree of life and the tree of the knowledge of good and evil. (Genesis 2:9) God instructed Adam and Eve not to eat the fruit from the tree of the knowledge of good and evil. Eating from that tree would allow death to enter the world. (Genesis 2:15-17) However, God did not want Adam and Eve to simply be robots. So, in His goodness and grace, God gave them the freedom of choice by creating them with a free will. He wanted them to choose to obey and love Him. Love is only love if it is freely chosen. They could choose to obey God's command or disobey it. At first they obeyed God's command, until the serpent changed Eve's mind.

"Now the serpent was more crafty than any other beast of the field that the Lord God had made." (Genesis 3:1) The serpent, possessed by the Devil (Satan), tempted Eve to question God's command. The serpent told her, "You will not surely die. For God knows that when you eat of it [the fruit] your eyes will be opened, and you will be like God, knowing good and evil." (Genesis 3:4, 5) Eve listened to the serpent's lies, and taking the fruit from the tree, she ate it. She also gave some to her husband Adam to eat. (Genesis 3:6) Then, sin, death, suffering, and evil entered the world because of their act of disobedience. Satan now had influence on the world, and it was no longer perfect. The perfect world became a broken world.

Satan was originally one of God's archangels. But Satan became proud and wanted to have God's role. One third of God's angels followed Satan. Satan's pride resulted in a war in Heaven against God and the angels who still followed Him. Satan and his angels (renamed as demons) lost. God cast Satan and his demons out of Heaven. (Isaiah 14:12-15)

After Adam and Eve disobeyed God, God came walking in the garden, calling to them. Adam and Eve were ashamed of their sin. God is a God of justice. Sin deserves punishment. God punished the serpent, the woman, and the man for their willful acts against Him. (Genesis 3:8-19) God had given humans the choice to live in a perfect world, but we wanted something more. As much as we like to blame Adam and Eve for starting all of the world's sins and sorrows, I believe anyone would have done the same thing, including me. They were humans just like us. As humans, we all sin by doing things that are wrong. Everyone in the world is sinful. No one is perfect except God. (Matthew 5:48) Romans 3:23 says, "For all have sinned and fall short of the glory of God." That word, "all" means everyone who ever lived and ever will live. It includes me too. The cost of sin is death, eternal separation from God. Romans 6:23 states, "For the wages of sin is death, but the free gift of God is eternal life in Christ Jesus our Lord."

But the story doesn't end with Adam and Eve's sin. God is a just God, but He is also a loving God. He had a plan for saving humans from sin. God sent His only son Jesus to come down to earth as a little baby. He was 100% God and 100% man. (Matthew 1:18-25) When Jesus grew up to be a man, He died on the cross for the sins of the entire world. (John 19:17-37) John 3:16 says, "For God so loved the world, that he gave his only Son, that whoever believes in him should not perish but have eternal life." But Jesus didn't stay dead. Three days after His death, He came back to life. After spending some time with those who had followed Him, He returned to Heaven. (John 20:1-10, Acts 1:1-11, I Corinthians 15:3-8)

Do you see it, dear reader? Those who believe in Jesus have eternal life with Him in Heaven. Romans 3:24-25 says, "[All] are justified by his grace as a gift, through the redemption that is in Christ Jesus, whom God put forward as a propitiation by his blood, to be received by faith." Propitiation means to regain good standing in a relationship with God. God loves the whole world and everyone who will ever live in it. That includes you! God loves you! He loves you so much that He sent His only Son Jesus to die on the cross for your sins. Because of Jesus Christ's death on the cross, all who ask to be forgiven can freely receive forgiveness from their sins. God offers eternal life in Heaven with Him to anyone who repents of their sin and acknowledges Jesus as the Savior and Lord of their life. (1 John 1:8-9, Romans 10:9-13) To those who receive Him as their Savior, He offers a relationship of comfort and protection while on this earth. (Psalm 23, John 14:27) That offer is open to you, dear reader.

As you can see, I put a lot of Bible verses in this section. That was intentional. I wanted to explain why I still say, "God is good." I say it because all these things written in the Bible are true. Jesus paid the price for my sins. He paid the price for the sins of the whole world after humans turned their back on His goodness. I believe that a God Who saved humans from the sin they allowed into the world is a GOOD God. This is the good God I willingly choose to serve. No trials or hardships in my life can ever change the fact that He is good. Nothing can ever change that fact.

WHY WOULD A SOVEREIGN GOD ALLOW BAD THINGS TO HAPPEN IN THE WORLD?

One assignment for my degree in Advanced Biblical Studies was writing a ten-page paper on the question, "Why Would God Allow Evil into the World?" This section reflects what I wrote in my paper and the conclusions I have come to over the years from reading my Bible, having a personal relationship with God, and reading other books. I realize I'm tackling a very big question, and there is more to the answer than what I provide here. I don't have all the answers to this question, but since my faith is part of my story, I wanted to share my beliefs on this question. The two main parts that I will address are God's sovereignty and evil.

Understanding God' sovereignty is very tough. I don't know if we can as humans actually fully and truly understand it. I'm only going to address a few facets of His sovereignty here. Sovereignty means having all authority. God has complete reign in this world and the power to carry out His plans. (Jeremiah 32:17 NIV) Therefore He is in control of all things. God is God, and we are not. That's the bottom line. God is the King and Ruler of this world. We are simply humans. So we can't rationalize and understand everything God does. If we could, I guess we would all be gods wouldn't we? Because God is sovereign, there are things in this life we won't understand. That's why He is God, and we are not. I understand this idea might make you angry. That's okay! There were times when it made me angry too. But as I understood it more, I was able to accept it. I challenge you to take the time to wrestle with God on this issue for yourself. Ask God to help you find an answer that satisfies you.

So, if God is sovereign, why does He allow bad things to

happen in this world? God originally created this world to be perfect. The perfect world reflected God's glory. But in Genesis 3, as I explained earlier, sin entered the world through Satan's temptation and Adam and Eve's disobedience against God. This answers the question of HOW evil came into the world. Humans brought it on themselves by believing Satan's lies.

So, why would a sovereign God ALLOW evil into the world? God created humans to love Him. Just as parents want their children to love them, God wants us to love Him, but He wants us to choose that love. Love that is not willingly chosen is not love. God did not create robots. He created humans with a free will. With a free will must come choices. When Adam and Eve chose to disobey, God let them make that choice. He allows us the same freedom today. We can choose to obey or disobey His commands. Everyone in the world has this choice. God allows evil in the world because He allows humans to have a free will. Some evil is the result of people's choices to disobey God's commands. Humans decided in the Garden of Eden that they knew better than God, and they continue to make that decision to this day. Although God is a sovereign, loving Ruler, we have to remember that sometimes God allows bad things to happen because He has given us the free will to choose right or wrong. I know it's a hard answer to accept. Ask God to help you understand it in a way that will satisfy you.

By believing the serpent, Adam and Eve helped start Satan's evil work in the world which he continues to this day. (I John 3:8, John 10:10, Ephesians 6:10-13) He is constantly tempting people to do wrong and giving them ideas how to do evil things. People have a choice to resist his temptations, but they often choose to listen to his evil ideas. (James 4:7, I Peter 5:8-9)

Sometimes God allows bad things to happen because He wants to draw people closer to Himself. This is true in my story. I found God and blessings and joy in the hard places in life more than in the good times. In countless ways along my journey, I saw

God remain my Rock and stand by my side. My life was hard, but it wasn't terrible. It was the best thing that happened to me. I'm able to see that now. I wasn't able to see that when I was going through all my hardships. During my hard times, I looked for God in my life, and I saw Him everywhere. I was looking for God because I needed Him more than ever before. (Psalm 73:28 NIV) I know there are thousands of other stories like mine where people found God in the midst of hardships. God is working, even during the hardest parts of life. It's like training for a marathon. The growth comes from hard work, not from sitting on a couch.

When life is easy, people often tend to forget about God. We get distracted by so many things in this world that just aren't important. Sometimes, God refocuses our eyes on what's important for life and eternity. For my story, God used the trials in my life to help mature me. We as humans often learn and mature through trials. There are some lessons we just don't seem to be able to learn the easy way. Athletes, students, and parents understand that concept. Achieving important things takes time, commitment, and endurance. So it is with faith. It takes time, growth, commitment, and endurance to grow in a relationship with God. It can be very hard but very rewarding. (Romans 5:3-5, James 1:2-4, 2 Corinthians 12:9) These lessons are not meant to be a punishment. They are meant to help us grow and mature in our relationship with God. However, not everything about faith in God is hard. There are some lessons that are learned in very sweet, special seasons with God when He woos our hearts with His passionate love. Those are beautiful lessons to experience!

Dear reader, if there are bad things happening in your life, it doesn't automatically mean that you did anything wrong to "deserve" them. Maybe there is something that God wants to teach you through them. In the midst of our hard times, He walks next to us and shows that He provides for our needs and cares for us. (Matthew 6:25-34, Matthew 7:7-11) For a miracle to happen there has to be a situation where only a miracle can fix it. Otherwise it's not a miracle! For God to show that He can provide for your needs there has to be a need for Him to fill. It doesn't mean God gives us everything we want, not even parents do that for their kids! God gives us what is best for us. He is looking out for our eternal life as well as our life here on earth. A deep faith is more important than our immediate and shallow "happiness." (I Peter 1:6, 7)

Another thing we must keep in mind is life after death. Everyone is going to live forever. It's up to them to decide where they spend their eternity. Will they spend eternity with God in Heaven? Or will they spend eternity apart from Him and utterly alone in Hell? For those who follow God, they have a wonderful life in Heaven to look forward to as an eternal reward for being faithful to God during their life on earth. Those faithful people have their names written in God's Book of Life. (Malachi 3:16-18) For those who don't follow God, they will be forever separated from God in Hell. (Revelation 20:11-15) God doesn't punish all the evil in the world right now. God will create a new earth someday. When this current earth is gone, God will judge all the evil that has been committed in the world. (Revelation 21:1-8) Everyone will give an account to God for how they lived their lives. (Matthew 12:36, 37) This earthly life is not all there is to life. We must keep eternity in mind.

We must also keep in mind the fact that sin has consequences. When someone speeds, they get pulled over by a police officer. That's not God's fault. It's a natural consequence of breaking the law. It works the same way with God's Law. When people don't follow His commands, there are natural consequences that follow from that disobedience and decision to live life their own way.

I realize this has been a heavy section, but I have good news for you! God can bring good out of horrible situations. Romans 8:28 states, "And we know that for those who love God all things work together for good, for those who are called according to his purpose." The verse does not say that all things *are good*. It says God can work all things together *for good* for those who love Him.

We can rest in the fact that He is working on our behalf. (Romans 8:31-32) God can take something horrible and make good come out of it. God doesn't *want* bad things to happen. That isn't the desire of His heart. But instead of overruling human choices, He chooses to make good come from the bad. God, in His vast mercy and love, did not leave humans alone to suffer in the evil they had let into the world. He provided a way of help and salvation in the midst of the evil. I explained earlier how He offers us a relationship with Him through believing in His Son Jesus.

Believing in God's sovereignty means trusting God to be faithful even if there is no explanation to what is happening in life. Trusting in God's sovereignty means believing that God is good even when you are surrounded by trials. Believing in His sovereignty is also realizing that God is bigger and better than anything you know or can imagine. I know that no matter what happens in life, I choose to serve God and recognize that He is the Ruler of my life. No matter what happens, God is my Ruler and His sovereign ways are perfect. Even if I would not choose those ways specifically, my sovereign God knows best!

MY RESPONSE TO WHAT HAS HAPPENED IN MY LIFE

The topic of why God would allow bad things to happen to me personally is somewhat hard to explain. Because it is my personal life story, it might not quite make sense to everyone. I explained earlier the reasons I found in the Bible to believe God is good. Because I believe God is good, I believe His plan for my life is good. It wasn't the plan I had in mind, but I wouldn't trade it for the plans I had made.

In God's perfect timing, He called Stephen home on April 27, 2013. In my eyes, the way Stephen went to Heaven was perfect. No one should feel guilty for Stephen's death. It was no one's fault that he had a heart condition. It was no one's fault that he went to play basketball that night. It was no one's fault that his heart didn't start again after it stopped. I firmly believe it was God's sovereign plan to call Stephen home that night.

It has taken time, but as I've been able to process what happened to me in the past several years, I'm able to see God's goodness and sovereignty in my life. When I got sick, there were so many unanswered questions about why I was sick. It was so hard to understand what God was doing. As time went on, the saying, "God is good," became a motto of Stephen's and my everyday life. On some hard days, I would weep, questioning why God was allowing me to be sick. Other days I found myself joyful in my pain because I was learning so much about God and living life well.

I don't believe God allowed me to go through hardships because He wanted to hurt me. I believe God is a loving God, and His plans for His children are good. I believe that what happened in my life has been made into something stunningly beautiful. I also believe it was the best plan for my life. Often after going through trials, we can see the beauty that comes from our brokenness.

I don't know all the reasons for everything I've experienced, but one of those reasons is you, dear reader. You certainly wouldn't be reading this book if Stephen were still alive and I was healthy. I also know I have had a greater impact on other peoples' lives because of my struggle with hardships.

Despite my sorrows, I can say with all sincerity, "God has used the hardships in my life for good!" Jeremiah 29:11 says, "For I know the plans I have for you, declares the LORD, plans for welfare and not for evil, to give you a future and a hope." You may wonder why I believe that. How could my sickness and Stephen's death be wonderful or glorious? Well my sickness and Stephen's death were not at all wonderful or glorious! But seeing how those hardships brought me and others closer to God was wonderful and glorious! They brought me closer to God than I've ever been. God brought good out of those hardships. He drew me and others closer to Himself and showed us more of His love.

Each and every day that I was experiencing a hard time, God was humbling and softening my heart toward him. I did not even realize how much I wanted to live life my own way before I got sick and Stephen died. My life was focused on the things of this world. I was planning what I wanted to do and who I wanted to become in life. But God's plans were "to give [me] a future and a hope." Let me explain something. Before I got sick, I was experiencing a wonderful time in life. However, I knew I didn't want to get too comfortable. I knew that people can grow and learn through difficult experiences. I saw myself becoming so comfortable that I didn't want anything to change. I saw myself starting to want the easy life. I also knew that if life were easy, I wouldn't always try harder to better myself or my relationship with God. So I prayed a simple yet hard prayer that summer in 2012. "Lord, humble my life and make me more like You. Take away my pride in the easy and hard times to see You as my forever salvation." (Colossians 3:2) God used the hardships of my life to humble me and make me more like Him.

It is like polishing a mirror so the reflection is clearer. God polished me with the hard times to make me a clearer reflection of His love and care for others.

I don't think that God sent me all those trials as an answer to my prayer. I think He took the trials I experienced and brought good out of them as an answer to my prayer. Sometimes when we ask for something, God uses the hardships we experience as an answer to our prayers. As I said earlier, bad things happen because of multiple different reasons, so sometimes God just takes the bad things that happen and recycles them into what we asked Him to teach us.

I am still struggling with the physical effects of my unforgettable sickness of severe migraines, sinus issues, iron deficiency, and other health problems, all caused from mold poisoning. I seldom had health problems before, and I questioned God as I struggled with a form of an auto-immune disease. I am now in year seven of my health journey. I don't fully understand why God allowed my sickness. But, as my loving Father, He knows what's best for me. It may not have always felt like it was the best thing for me. But looking back from where I am now, I can see He has brought so much good out of it all. As I sit here writing and thinking, I realize, with fresh tears in my eyes, that God answered the prayer I prayed the summer I got sick. My struggles have humbled me and have made me hunger for God more than ever before. My God is God. My God is Sovereign. My God is so good! (Psalm 145:1)

I learned that God never wants to hurt me. When I'm sad, He's sad. He hurts when I am hurting. He grieves with me when I grieve. I also came to understand that God can do anything in His sovereignty. He could have made a way that I didn't get sick. He could have. But God did something else. I got sick, and that wasn't because God caused it. I believe God used my sickness and circumstances to draw me closer to Him as I sought after Him.

Why would God allow Stephen to die before we got married? Why would God take such a young person? I don't know the answer. But I know that He is sovereign, and His way is better than my way. I may not always like this answer. It doesn't offer a nice, satisfying answer to the "whys" I ask. But it is still true. I don't believe I will ever come to a point where all my hurt and suffering suddenly "makes sense." But I am learning to see good come from my suffering. Do I miss Stephen? Yes! Am I content to live on earth without Stephen? It has taken me awhile to come to this answer, but the answer is, "YES!" I will see Stephen again one day when I go to Heaven.

God's plan for me is something wonderful, and I plan to live out my passions and my mission to serve God to my fullest capacity. I have come to a place where I can accept God's sovereign plan in my life. I don't fully understand why He has chosen to allow everything that happened, but I am confident it won't ruin His wonderful plan for my life. Because I believe God is good, I know His plan for my life is good, the very best, for me. (2 Samuel 7:28 NIV)

God's plan is so perfect! Do you believe that? Whether you believe it or don't believe it or maybe you're learning to believe it, my prayer is that one day you will come to know the amazing God Who created the world, Who loves His children with an unconditional and self-sacrificial love, and Who has a plan that is better than ours. Stephen Reynolds was part of God's glorious plan. Who am I to challenge God's perfect plan and to ask Him to change it for my selfish gain? When Stephen died, I mourned and cried because I had lost the man whom I was going to marry, my best friend in the world, and a great man of God. He was gone from this world. I would never see him again on this earth, laugh with him, hug him, pray with him, cry with him, have our first kiss, go on walks, or enjoy his smile. I know that God has a plan and purpose for taking Stephen home before I wanted. God can take the worst circumstances in our lives to show the world His glory, splendor, and love. I learned after Stephen died that in suffering and death, God can be glorified. People came to know God and were closer to Him because of Stephen's death. That's why I believe that in Stephen's death God was glorified. The God of the universe, Who knows everything, knew that this would be best for us.

What about you? Your story is not the same as mine. You can also probably tell a tale of hardships you have experienced. Have you asked God the same question I did? "God, why would You allow bad things to happen to me?" Maybe you are still struggling with God's answer or what seems to be the lack of an answer. I want you to know, God does love you. Yes, you! Life is not easy. It never has been (except in Eden) and never will be until Heaven. The Bible shows us this truth. (John 16:33)Yet, God is in total control, and He is sovereign. My God, our God, is good!

I'd like to end with this idea. Asking, "Why would God allow bad things to happen to me," is not bad. Asking and questioning during times of intense sorrow is normal. It's okay to tell God what's on our hearts. He already knows. He just wants us to acknowledge it. As we allow God to heal our hearts, gradually the questioning and asking goes away. However, we cannot bring about our own healing. We have to ask God to come and heal our hearts for us and allow Him to do it. Throughout my healing process, I came to realize something. God allowed me to go through hard times in order to teach me things I did not know. He did this so I could draw closer to Him, become more mature in my faith, and fall more in love with Him. He grieved with me when I became sick and lost my health. He grieved with me when I lost Stephen. He grieved with me many other times along this journey. God has always been there for me, every step of the way, providing what I needed. I sit in awe of Him. He is holy, loving, caring, and sovereign. My God, whom I willingly serve and trust, is worthy of all praise.

What about you, dear reader? Where do you find your healing from the hurts of this world? If you aren't a Christian, I hope this book has at least stirred your curiosity to learn more about God. Look at the resource section in the back of this book if you would like more information about Christianity. If you are a Christian, I hope this book has encouraged and inspired you in your journey of following God.

REFLECTION OF HOPE

Hope. Everyone is looking for hope. Sometimes hope can seem so far away. When calamities strike, tears fall, and troubles entangle our lives, we look for hope. Many times when I find myself searching for hope, I look up. If it's light outside, I look at the sky, the clouds and the sun. If it's dark outside, I look at the moon and stars (always trying to find the Big Dipper). Sometimes I just stare into the darkness of the night.

In the midst of everything I faced during those several hard years, I struggled to find hope when the trials became overwhelming. I sought after the only thing that made sense to me, Jesus. He gave me hope, joy, and purpose on the hardest days. Yet, there were still days when life was so hard I wondered if hope was worth it.

I have thought a lot about hope since my losses. If you've gone through hardships you know what I mean. When life becomes hard you wonder if you are making the right decisions on how to handle life. I wondered at times if my hope in God was worth it. When I was so broken, I saw so many broken people around me. But they were handling their brokenness differently from the way I was. I wondered if any of their choices gave them hope. I wondered if I should try their ideas. However, in all my ponderings, I always concluded that hope in God was the only thing that made sense. Deep down I knew I could never give up my faith in God. My faith was, and is, such a huge part of my life that giving up my faith would mean giving up part of myself.

In the spring of 2013, before Stephen died, God gave me a dream that gave me hope. (This was not a vision like the ones I had while I lay unconscious, while I was in surgery, and while I was in the ER. This was just a vivid dream I had one night.)

I had a dream,
I dreamed that I was talking to God.
"It's so hard," I cried out to him, as He sat and talked to me.
Jesus came and held my hand.
The pain was so unbearable,
But Jesus told me great things were to come in my perseverance.
The next part of the dream,
I was on earth, living in my pain.
I was on the ground and heard laughter above me.
Looking up, I saw three demons looking down upon me, laughing.
I began to cry, moan in pain, and called out for help!
"Jesus, help me," I called.
In response to my call,
He answered, "I've been here all along. You've
been trying to do this on your own."

This dream gave me hope because it reminded me that Jesus is always with me and is walking alongside me. I didn't have to face these trials on my own. He was there to help me, even when I couldn't see Him.

During these difficult times of loss, I went on a search to discover more of what the word "hope" means. I discovered that there is no greater hope than hope in God. I Peter 1:18-21 says, "knowing that you were ransomed…with the precious blood of Christ…so that your faith and hope are in God." Hope goes hand-in-hand with faith. Without faith, hope just becomes wishful thinking, which doesn't get very far. Also faith without hope is empty. Why have faith if what you believe in offers no hope? But when hope is coupled with faith in God it becomes an action plan and guide for life. We can live out our faith because we have hope that God is faithful to those who follow Him. He will provide, care for, guide, comfort, and direct those who follow Him. His good plan for His children will prevail.

I saw all this in my journey. God was always there for me. My faith gave me hope that He would care for me, just like it says in the Bible. That's the best kind of hope, hope in God. If my hope is in God, I don't need to look any further. Anything else that I put my hope in will eventually crumble and fall.

Hope in God also takes away my fear of death. I know that when it is my time to die, I will join God in Heaven for all eternity. Not many people like to think about death. For some they think more about *how* they will die. Others think about life after death and where they will go, Heaven or Hell. What an important subject! For some it could be a joyful occasion. For others it could be utter misery. If you know you're going to go to Heaven, then do not fear the *how*, for Jesus said "My grace is sufficient for you, for my power is made perfect in weakness." (2 Corinthians 12:9). For those whose hope is in Christ, right after death, you will be with the Lord and will not remember any pain, troubles, or fears! The Lord is good to those who put their hope in Him. For those who have no hope in God, they should fear death. They should fear pain. For when they die they will live their life in the pit of Hell, far from anything beautiful, joyful, or loving. (Matthew 10:28, Luke 16:19-31)

So, I write to you, dear reader, and reemphasize that hope in God is ALWAYS worth it. I don't know where you are in your life's journey. Maybe you're looking for something to cling to. I encourage you to seek after God and cling to Him. He will be the greatest hope you will ever know. Even on the hardest days, hope in God will help you through more than you can imagine. Faith in God's goodness gives us hope!

The definitions that people use for the word hope intrigue me. People use the word hope all the time. Just listen to a person's vocabulary and hear how many times they say the word hope. So I ask you, do you have hope? Where is your hope? And who is your hope in?

CHAPTER 18

Romans 15:13
May the God of hope fill you with all joy and
peace in believing, so that by the power of the
Holy Spirit you many abound in hope.

OVERCOMING HARD TIMES

If you are looking for a simple answer to fix your hard times, I say to you, "You're reading the wrong book!" I don't have the "fix it manual" for life. However, I do have an answer of hope. In Matthew 5:3-12, Jesus told these words to the crowds of people gathered around Him.

> "Blessed are the poor in spirit, for theirs is the kingdom of heaven.
> "Blessed are those who mourn, for they shall be comforted.
> "Blessed are the meek, for they shall inherit the earth.
> "Blessed are those who hunger and thirst for righteousness, for they shall be satisfied.
> "Blessed are the merciful, for they shall receive mercy.

"Blessed are the pure in heart, for they shall
see God.
"Blessed are the peacemakers, for they shall be
called sons of God.
"Blessed are those who are persecuted for
righteousness' sake, for theirs is the kingdom of
heaven.
"Blessed are you when others revile you and
persecute you and utter all kinds of evil against
you falsely on my account. Rejoice and be glad,
for your reward is great in heaven, for so they
persecuted the prophets who were before you."

Jesus called each of these people blessed. Read that again.
Is that not amazing! Blessed are the poor in spirit. Blessed are
those who mourn. Blessed are the meek. Blessed are the hungry.
Blessed are the merciful. Blessed are the pure in heart. Blessed are
those who are persecuted for righteousness' sake, and blessed are
those persecuted for the name of Christ. Jesus will bless you in
the middle of your hard times! Isn't that incredible! There is true,
beautiful hope in hard times! Blessed – you are blessed! If that
does not bring you hope and encouragement, I don't know what
will. Keep your eyes fixed on Jesus Christ and take life one step at
a time. Jesus Christ is your only HOPE! He is the answer to your
heart's deepest questions and longings.

Many days, I would pour over this Scripture crying from literal
pain while reading, "Blessed are those who mourn, for they shall
be comforted." Then I would move down a few verses and read,
"Blessed are the pure in heart, for they shall see God." One day,
that phrase, "the pure in heart" really stopped me. It was a heart
check within me. I literally looked around to see if anyone was
near me. I had been complaining earlier that morning before
reading these verses. God knew my complaints, my hardships,
and my grumblings. He had heard me. With that phrase, God

reminded me that I must honor Him in all I do. "Blessed are the pure in heart, for they shall see God." God wasn't going to honor my whining, complaining and grumbling. However, He would honor a thankful heart. He would even honor honest questions asked from a heart willing to accept His answers, even if that answer was silence. As children of God, we are called to honor Him at all times, in all things. Are you willing to glorify God in all things at all times? (Colossians 3:17) Are you willing to accept the hope Jesus offers to you in the above verses? How do you overcome your hard times?

Everyone is trying to overcome something in their life. Traumatic events come upon us that sometimes we do not know how to handle. Maybe you can relate to my story of trauma and trials, or maybe you cannot. You may have a story of trying to overcome alcohol or drug addiction, lust, gossip, abuse, anger, gluttony, homelessness, lack of finances, losing your job, being persecuted for the name of Jesus, hardships in dating, or hardships in friendships and family relationships. Maybe you are trying to overcome fear, lack of love, depression, or trust issues. You are not alone. If you ask God to come and help you overcome it, He will.

What are the hard times that you have gone through? What are the emotions, the fears, and the blessings? Write them down! You don't want to forget your journey and how far God has brought you. I encourage you to keep a record of some kind. It will allow you to see how God is working in your life even when it's hard. As you go through life, you can then look back and see how God has provided for you all along the way. You can journal a few simple words or many words. Whatever you do, do not forget God's goodness!

LIFE'S JOURNEY

As a woman close to thirty, I know I look at life differently than someone older than I am. I know that 50 years from now, I will look back on this part of my life through the eyes of other growing experiences I will have encountered. Life keeps going. Joyful occasions happen. Hardships come upon us, but God's comfort, grace and sovereignty never change.

The loss of a dear loved one is inevitable. Death is a part of life in this broken world. Grief is hard. It is good to allow ourselves to cry tears of sorrow, loss, and grief, but we must not stay in that grief forever. The memory of our loved ones lives on in us. Remember the good times, and don't dwell on the bad memories.

Hard times will make you go on a journey, but it is your choice which road you will take. You can journey toward the things you think will satisfy your soul, or you can journey toward a new relationship with Jesus Christ or a deeper relationship with Him. Jesus says, "Come to me, all who labor and are heavy laden, and I will give you rest." (Matthew 11:28) You don't have to go through life on your own. I have already shared the good news of Jesus's death on the cross for your sins. Now it is up to you to decide what you will do with that information. If you already trust Jesus as your Savior, remember that you are not alone. Call on your Father, the God of Heaven and earth when you are in need. Remember you have brothers and sisters in Christ whom God has sent to be with you, pray with you, and support you through the rough times. Reach out to them and tell them specifically how they can support you.

We each have a story. Each of us has a journey in life, just like the character named Christian in the book *The Pilgrim's Progress*. Sometimes it's easy to get bogged down and forget the good things when so many hard things come upon you. It's possible to forget about the goodness of God.

Personally, I look at life as an adventure, but that's just my perspective. How do you look at life? Life is hard, but is that where you put your focus? Is that your attitude? If you always view life as being hard, it will always be hard. A different perspective would be viewing life as a journey where sometimes really hard things happen. Yet, in spite of all the hard times, there are many days when you will still laugh. You will still smile, and you will still enjoy life. That is the journey of life! Life isn't lived all in one wonderful or hard experience. It's a journey that takes a lifetime of experiences.

Everything takes time. Grief is a process. Going through hardships and overcoming them is a process, but God will help you through your hard times. (Matthew 7:7-8) God will send people into your life to encourage you and build you up. Through Stephen's and my story, I hope you have seen how good God is, for surely God is good! May God bless you as you live your life! May you find blessings in the hard times! May you be able to say in the middle of your struggles, "God is good!" God is good, even when life is hard!

PART 3
TYING IT ALL TOGETHER

CHAPTER 19

Ecclesiastes 3:1-17
"For everything there is a season, and a time
for every matter under heaven:
a time to be born, and a time to die;
a time to plant, and a time to pluck up what is planted;
a time to kill, and a time to heal;
a time to break down, and a time to build up;
a time to weep, and a time to laugh;
a time to mourn, and a time to dance;
a time to cast away stones, and a time
to gather stones together;
a time to embrace, and a time to refrain from embracing;
a time to seek, and a time to lose;
a time to keep, and a time to cast away;
a time to tear, and a time to sew,
a time to keep silence, and a time to speak;
a time to love and a time to hate;
a time for war, and a time for peace.*
What gain has the worker from his toil? I have seen the business
that God has given to the children of man to be busy with. He
has made everything beautiful in its time. Also, he has put
eternity into man's heart, yet so that he cannot find out what
God has done from the beginning to the end. I perceived that
there is nothing better for them than to be joyful and to do good

as long as they live; also that everyone should eat and drink and take pleasure in all his toil – this is God's gift to man.

I perceived that whatever God does endures forever; nothing can be added to it, nor anything taken from it. God has done it, so that people fear before him. That which is, already has been; that which is to be, already has been; and God seeks what has been driven away."

FACTS

I want to list some facts about grief and sickness. Sometimes grief and sickness can seem similar. Sometimes they feel very different. Whether you have endured the death of a loved one, experienced sickness, or endured other hardships, the reality is that the pain is very real. People don't enjoy talking about the reality of hard times. Sometimes people don't like admitting how deep the pain is and how much it is affecting everything in their lives. However, when life feels most difficult, the Lord stands by our side, whispering, "Allow me take care of you, my child." This is the reality, dear reader, for those who follow God. I personally experienced it in my life. Even when life felt unbearable, I knew God was walking with me, holding me in His loving arms, carrying me through whatever I was experiencing.

Facts about Grief

- Grief is very hard to bear. Without God, grief is much, much harder to bear.
- When you lose someone close to you, there is much sorrow and sadness. Sometimes there are many tears. Sometimes the grief cannot be expressed.
- Many loved ones surround you soon after your loved one passes away.
- Sometimes you feel forgotten by your friends and family as you walk through your grief. Remember, they are *not*

intentionally shutting you out. They have their own lives to keep living. Sometimes they don't know how to help you live your new life. However, they still love you and want to support you. For those truly safe people who really want to help you, reach out and tell them practical ways they can help you.

- You are not alone. God is there for you during whatever you experience, wherever you are.
- You are loved by your friends and family. They may not always be able to express it in a way that you can understand, but they still love you.
- Sometimes you only want back what has been taken from you, even if it's impossible. There were times when I just wanted Stephen back. That was all I wanted. God can help you accept the loss of what is gone.
- Words sometimes aren't necessary. Sometimes a hug or a physical presence is all you need for someone to comfort you.
- You still need your friends, even if they don't understand what you are experiencing. If you are the friend of a hurting person, it's okay if you don't understand what they are experiencing. But keep supporting and loving that hurting person.
- You need extra love and support for at least a year from your friends and family. Birthdays, holidays, and sometimes even weekends are just hard.
- •When your loved one dies, your world stops, even though the rest of the world seems to continue going forward.
- You need to talk about your loved one, and you need others to listen. Sometimes people do not know how to handle hearing you talk about someone who has died. They find it uncomfortable. Talking about your loved one is hard, but it is also good for you. Find the people who are willing to talk about your loved one with you.

Facts about Having a Daily, Long-term Sickness

- You don't want to be sick, and no one wants you to be sick. Only through Jesus Christ can you find peace in accepting your sickness.

- Your friends and family may not know how to respond to your sickness over a long period of time. They might continue to tell you, "Get well soon," even if the reality is you may never get better.

- Some people may offer suggestions and advice on how to get well. They only do that because they want you to get well. Sometimes their suggestions are not helpful. Ask God to help you be gracious in responding to these suggestions.

- You would love to be like everyone else! You would love to climb mountains, run marathons, play sports, and live like you used to. Maybe you'd like to enjoy something you used to do all the time or to pursue your passions again without them exhausting you. Maybe you can't even do your own laundry anymore or make your own meals. I understand the frustration of feeling helpless. However, as I've cried about my inabilities, God has picked me up and given me strength for other things I *can* do while I'm sick. Whether I'm sick for the rest of my life or not, I am awed and blessed by my great God's provision!

- It takes a very special friend to be with a sick person for the long haul. Some friends would like to be there more often for you, but they don't know how.

- Your recreational abilities change. Find things that you can still do with others. Sitting and chatting, watching movies, or driving were some simple things I was able to find enjoyment in when I was sick. Just because you can't do what you used to do doesn't mean you can't do anything fun.

- You sleep a lot! Your body needs that sleep.
- Being sick is very humbling. Asking for help daily is very hard. Your pride kicks you in places you never even knew you had pride. Allow the Lord to use it to humble you.
- Whether you get better or not, you have to keep up a positive attitude. Make God your first priority. Seek Him daily in the Bible. Daily count your blessings.
- My story is real. So is yours. But our stories are not over yet. Allow God to write your story.

These facts are not written just to those who have lost a loved one or to someone who is sick. They are written to all those who have gone through hard times.

REALITY

I wrote the poem "Reality" one year after Stephen's death. I wrote it to help me process through my grief. It truly did help me process and grieve.

The reality is, the truth is, the fact is
That both grief and sickness are hard
The reality is, the truth is, the fact is
When life gets hard you sometimes just want to give up.
The reality is, the truth is, the fact is
"What if my life," keeps playing in your head like a record. "What if my life continues to be hard," never stops playing.
The reality is, the truth is, the fact is
"What is this world about? What am I living my life for?" These, my friends, become daily questions when life calamities strike.
The reality is, the truth is, the fact is
I'm lonely. I think, deep down, you're lonely too. Deep down, you're lonely and trying to fill your loneliness with things that you think will make you "happy." Things such as food, money, technology,

cars, sinful desires, media, substance abuse, even people. What if those things, your loves of this world, were taken from you!? Only when I find contentment in my life, when I am content in Jesus Christ, will my loneliness then be filled. The same is true for you. Find contentment in Jesus Christ, and He will satisfy you.

The reality is, the truth is, the fact is

I am very blessed; you are very blessed; we are very blessed.

The reality is, the truth is, the fact is

There is a time for everything; a time to laugh, a time to cry, a time to be born, and a time to die. All of this is for the glory of God! Reality is, truth is, fact is, we all need God. Without Him we lack everything, let us glorify His name!

Truth is, there is a time for everything.

Some people die young while some people die old. That is reality.

Truth is, life is hard.

Some people see their cup of life half full while others see their cup of life half empty.

Who are you?

Whether you have 5 minutes, 5 hours, 5 years, or 50 more years to live

What are you living your seconds, minutes, hours, and years for?

Who are you living them for?

What is your purpose in life?

Who has God created you to be?

Can you answer that?

Because, the reality is, the truth is, the fact is, we all are searching for something, for a deeper purpose in our lives. When calamities come, we look for reality; we look for truths; we look for facts that point us to that deeper meaning and purpose in life.

Reality is

Truth is

Fact is

God is real, and He created you for something beautiful.

The reality is, everyone fears death.
Heaven is beautiful, but Hell is utter misery.
Reality is, everyone hates pain.
Mankind strives for happiness.
Reality is, everyone wants to be happy.
Truth is, everyone needs someone.
All humans need hugs.
Truth is, everyone longs for love.
Fact is, without God life is miserable.
Reality is, truth is, fact is
God's love is real.
God's Word is truth.
Jesus's death and resurrection are real facts.
Reality is, truth is, fact is
Life is hard, and God is good!

CHAPTER 20

Philippians 1:3-5, 7a
I thank my God in all my remembrance of you, always
in every prayer of mine for you all making my prayer
with joy, because of your partnership in the gospel from
the first day until now...It is right for me to feel this
way about you all, because I hold you in my heart....

MEMORIES OF STEPHEN FROM
THE REYNOLDS FAMILY

The Reynolds are an incredible family. The whole family enjoys sports, loves to spend time together, and has an amazing faith in Jesus Christ. Here are their stories of memories with Stephen, of laughter that was shared, and even of hard times after the sudden shock of Stephen's death.

Mr. Reynolds is the head of the family and takes care of his family through the good and bad times. His firm foundation is the Lord Almighty Who holds him steadfastly. Mrs. Reynolds is the first lady of this family. She makes sure all her children are doing well and watches out for them during their journeys in life. Mrs. Reynolds is a prayer warrior who never gives up hope. Chris is the oldest of the Reynolds children. He has a fun personality, enjoys basketball, and loves a good laugh. Chris also is the big brother who would do anything to take care of his younger siblings. He has three sweet, adorable children of his own, Neveah, Chris Jr., and Moriah. They have amazing imaginations, lots of energy, spunk and creativity, and are the sweetest, most adorable kids I know.

Anthony is the second oldest child. He may be a bit quiet as a first impression, but he is a jokester who loves to laugh. Anthony loves video games and sports like most guys do. Stephen was next in line after Anthony. Aundra is the youngest child and the only girl. She is spunky, loves to write, and enjoys the game of basketball just like the rest of her family. There is a close bond between the siblings, and they check up on each other throughout the weeks and months. Although Stephen and I were never married, the Reynolds family still feels like my family. I love them so much!

MR. ANTHONY REYNOLDS SR.

Mon the Man (Mr. Reynolds' nickname for Stephen)

Stephen Phillip Reynolds was born January 31, 1990, and was named Stephen by his mother and Phillip by his father's mother. These are the same names of the first two men chosen out of seven men in the book of Acts who were later called deacons. I think it is only fitting that his names are the first two mentioned in the church of Jerusalem pertaining to the act of service. Stephen, in the book of Acts, was known for his ability to stand up and debate. The Bible says the Pharisees could not stand against his wisdom or the spirit by which he spoke. Let me tell you, Stephen Reynolds was much the same because he and I had many debates about many things. He always had his facts straight and never resorted to embellishment to make his points stronger. Phillip fit him also, for he was not afraid to evangelize. He was also like Phillip in the Bible because when he was out of school and out of church he did not consider that time as "time off." He evangelized my neighbor across the street during said "off" time. My neighbor personally told me that he began to attend church again after Stephen talked to him. Like Phillip, who was moved to talk to the Ethiopian eunuch, Stephen saw his free time as the LORD'S TIME. Yes, Stephen and Phillip were correct names for him.

We found out later that Stephen was born with a heart murmur. As parents we pondered what that would mean but did not feel any anxiety. As an infant, he hardly ever cried and slept a lot. We thought, "What a wonderful baby." But as he grew older, we noticed he was tired easily, and he still slept a lot. We became concerned and took him to see a doctor. That was when we discovered the heart murmur.

As was his going-home celebration, so was his surgery. People from all over, from different churches, different denominations, and different families gathered with us at the hospital to give their support. After the surgery the doctor told us, "I have never performed that type of surgery that went as smoothly and as quickly and as well as this one did." Oh! The prayers of the saints! Oh! The grace of our God!

After the surgery and after his recovery, Stephen seemed to have a new surge of unlimited power and energy. It got to the point where I exclaimed to Naomi, "Maybe we ought to take him back and get the old heart back!" (Of course I said it as a joke.)

One time he came in our room late, near bedtime, climbed up into our bed and demanded, "Chris and Anthony have a TV and video games in their room and me and Aundra have nothing. And we want to know what ya are going to do about it!" He matter-of-factly got out of our bed and went to his room with complete confidence that he had made his point clear. I looked at Naomi and said, "These new heart neurons think they're tough don't they?" Once again I stated, "Maybe we ought to go get that old heart back." (He never had a heart transplant. It was just part of the joke.)

When Stephen was about five years old, he began to gain a love for basketball. I purchased a four-foot high basket for him at that time. He loved to play with that thing. He never shot jump shots. When he retrieved the ball, he would always go all the way to the goal and dunk it. I have always wondered how good a ballplayer he would have been had he not had that heart problem. Who knows?

The doctors instructed us that he was not to play organized sports or to play to the point of exhaustion and to keep an eye on him. They also said with his condition he would have to have that surgery three more times before he turned 18. However, each time we went back, the growth on his aorta valve did not show up like the doctors thought it would. The last time we went, the nurse practitioner looked on the screen and told the doctor who was sitting across the room, "It's not there." In disbelief, the doctor rolled his chair across the floor over to the screen, (not believing the nurse), gazed at the screen for a few moments, turned around, and looked at us with this puzzled look on his face and said, "It hasn't grown back." From then on we stopped going back.

After that we allowed him to play and even be on the basketball team at school. He ran up and down the court and played okay. But I just had a concern in my heart that he seemed more tired than he should have been. So I decided we ought to stop him from playing.

Stephen and I had a special relationship where we communicated very well. I think it stemmed from the fact that we were forced to spend a lot of time together.

When he was recovering, we didn't want to send him to a babysitter. I kept him with me until about 2:00 P.M. every day for a few months and dropped him off at Naomi's job around 2:00 P.M. if she could have him there. During that time, he was able to see me at work and at home. So he really knew me, and I really knew him. He was quiet, very well behaved, and very respectful to me and my clients. I think that is why he, more than his siblings, was able to approach me with anything he had on his mind. (This was the Lord's doing.) Even when he sinned and lost his virginity he came to me about it. Although I know his relationship with

Jesus Christ had a lot to do with his honesty, he still came to me. Without going into too much detail, he came to me with his head down, with bitter tears like Peter when he denied the Lord, with authentic brokenness, and with cracked speech, he confessed his sin. He told me even though he was not caught in the act, and no one else had told me. "A broken and contrite spirit, O God, thou wilt not despise." (Psalm 51:17 KJV) It made me love him more than if he had never committed the offense. I saw God and his love toward me and his children, and I felt God's love inside of me. Because he came to me with it and in the manner in which he came, it made me want to forgive him of any and all things he had ever done. As the father of the prodigal son, I felt so much love inside for him that I wanted to also throw a party for him to show him that even though he did what he did there is NOTHING between us to keep us from each other! At that moment I thought, "This is my youngest boy. He really knows and loves God! For this was on all accounts godly repentance."

While growing up, Stephen couldn't play sports and be athletically inclined, but he accepted it. That is one thing I want to proclaim about Mon. When he realized that things would not be what he wanted or that his life would not be like others' lives, he had the uncanny ability to accept his lot in life. So many of us take years to reach the kind of maturity of no complaints and no, "It's not fair statements." He just accepted it. He even told his brothers, "I don't have to play sports. I'm a genius!" He therefore applied that energy to his school work as a transition to his high school days.

Stephen was a very good student. He was accepted into Sumner Academy, the highest academic level of high schools in the Kansas City public school system. He never got into trouble in high school, and he always kept his grades up. He did not venture into the nightlife of his peers. Even in the summertime he was home with us every night and did not stay out late and party.

During his teenage years there was never any rebellion against his parents. There were no disrespectful conversations or blowups, not one. The only offense he had toward me was in becoming a spurs fan. Even after I raised him up as a Laker! I even bought him a No #32 Magic Johnson jersey, which he wore proudly. Then somewhere in his life he ventured into heathenville and somehow became a spurs fan. (spurs is not capitalized on purpose.) I have since learned to forgive him, and I too, now (believe it or not) cheer for them too.

In his college days, things didn't start off too well. But as time went on, his vexation with the lifestyles of his peers became too much to bear. Like Lot in Sodom and Gomorrah, it vexed his righteous soul. Like the Word of God says, "Don't be deceived, evil communications corrupt good character." (I Corinthians 15:33 paraphrased).

After the second year of college, he stayed home and took care of his brother's children, treating them as his own. He disciplined them with love and taught them to behave. I have no doubt he would have been a great father. He gave up a whole year to do this. He never once complained, nor did he seek compensation. He just did it and did it cheerfully. Neveah, the oldest, accepted Jesus Christ as her Lord and Savior at the tender age of seven years old. This is mainly because of Stephen's influence on her. They all ask me questions about Heaven now that they know Stephen is there. I don't think they would be as inquisitive about Heaven if it were not for Stephen's life and subsequent passing.

In his spiritual life, he was consistent, as in all other areas. I guess that made the other areas the way they were. I put this last because it is most important and explains the former. One day he asked me, "Dad, what does it mean, 'faithful are the wounds of a friend'?" (Proverbs 27:6 KJV) I explained it to him, and he understood. He took it and ran with it. He understood that if you really care about someone, you will tell them the truth about themselves even if it hurts. I know he had to read the other verse that comes before it. "Open rebuke is better than secret love."

(Proverbs 27:6) In other words, it's better to tell someone they're wrong upfront then to think, "I don't want to hurt their feelings, so I just won't say anything. I will just pray that God will speak to them about it." No, he knew and understood that if you know, you should tell them and keep them from heading into a path of destruction. Boy, did he ever take heed to those verses in Proverbs 27:5-6. He confronted me, his mother, his brothers and sister on different occasions. But let me reiterate, he also did it with love and concern and always with respect.

Appropriately, I will discuss the final chapter of his life on his relationship with Katie. He came to me with deep concern on how he should treat her. He never asked me for advice about any other female, only Katie. I noticed his countenance and moods had changed during the days before he asked me. I thought it was just being at Calvary Bible College. But it was more than just that. He had stepped over the equator line at Calvary where the climate and atmosphere change into Calvary BRIDAL College!! Once again, he came to me for advice. You can tell when a man has found the right woman for himself. Because when a man finds the woman he loves and wants to spend the rest of his life with, he does not want to make any mistakes. Everything I told him to do, he did, trusting my judgment. Also, after the days in which he was in Heaven, I found several books on marriage and pre-marriage that I did not know he had. I didn't read those kinds of books until years after I was married. Stephen was trying to be the right man for the right woman that God had blessed him with. He even told me he was going to pop the question. Even after the first meeting with her, I knew that his "early in a man" wisdom had led him to the right person. Maybe it's because I am old. Ha, ha!

I don't yet understand God's reason for taking him away so early, but this I do know, God never does things in his purpose to hurt us on purpose. Everything he does is contained in his purpose for those he loves and those that love him. And one day we WILL KNOW AS WE ARE KNOWN.

I didn't want him to go before me. But this I know! God loves Stephen more than I could ever comprehend. God wanted him to be with him before I did. God has done more for Stephen where he is now than I could ever have done for him in 100 lifetimes. So, Praise the Lord. The Lord giveth and the Lord taketh away. Blessed be the name of the LORD! (Job 1:21 paraphrased)

MRS. NAOMI REYNOLDS

Stephen's Mom

Stephen was born on a very cold day in January 1990. He grew and developed into a wonderful little boy. However, he routinely suffered with colds and sore throats. In 1996, he had a cold, and I took him to the doctor. The doctor told me that he would get over the cold, but he had another serious concern. His heart rate was not good. We set an appointment at Children's Mercy Hospital with the cardiologist which lasted all day.

The cardiologist had a team of specialists to discuss Stephen's case. It was decided that he would need open heart surgery because he had a heart disease called aortic stenosis. Everything was scheduled for Stephen to have the procedure done in the spring of 1996. The day of the surgery was long. Before he went in for the procedure, I gave him a scripture written on a piece of paper that said, "When I'm afraid I will trust in the Lord." (Psalm 56:3 *paraphrased*)

The ICU nurse would come out periodically and give an update. The surgery took about five hours. God blessed Stephen by letting him come through the surgery without any problems. We were so thankful to God, because He heard our prayers. Prayers from the east to the west were for him and our family. The hardest part was, because of the type of heart disease he had, he would require more surgery. God worked that out also. He didn't have to have another procedure done.

He was in the hospital for about four days. He didn't mind because at Children's Mercy Hospital they care for the children as if they are number one.

As time went on, he entered Hazel Grove Elementary School. His teachers loved him. He was an ideal student. Needless to say, parent-teacher conference was a breeze. Then came Coronado Middle School. He continued to strive to be a good student, but peer pressure would show up. He would be challenged because it was not cool to be smart and a young man.

Stephen overcame the pressure and graduated with honors from middle school. Along with graduating with honors, Stephen had a great love for the trumpet. In fact, he was so good that he earned the right for first chair in the band.

At the end of his eighth-grade year, he was asked to take the entrance exam for Sumner Academy. He was accepted, but Sumner proved to be a challenge for him. All of his friends went in as eighth graders, and he went in as a freshman, which was not good. He became very discouraged and did not apply himself. His GPA fell to a 2.4. To stay at Sumner one had to maintain a 2.5. He left Sumner and enrolled into F.L. Schlagle, home of the Marching Stallions. Schlagle was an "okay" situation for him because he was much more advanced. During his sophomore year, he was an honor student. This continued until he graduated in 2008. Stephen was in the Forensic Club and National Honor Society.

In the summer of 2007, I was diagnosed with ovarian cancer. Stephen and Aundra had just gotten back from summer camp. Before I went in for the surgery, Stephen prayed for me and the team of surgeons. He also prayed that the Lord would heal me completely.

In the summer of 2007, Stephen and his sister had the opportunity to attend a Christian Sports Camp called Kids Across America. All I can say is, "Wow." He came back a changed man. He was more intentional about reading his Bible and spending quiet time with the Lord. He would just pour himself into God's word.

In the fall of 2009, he entered Allen County Community College with a major in Physical Therapy. He planned to finish the two years at Allen and pursue a degree in sports medicine. However, God had another plan for Stephen's life. He actually took a year off, which was great because his older brother needed his help. Stephen's nieces and nephew moved in with us for a year, so he loved them and took very good care of them. Stephen would work nights, then come home and watch them until I got home from work. That was a great sacrifice, and Christ would reward him later for doing that. Nevaeh, Chris Jr. and Moriah loved Uncle Steve dearly.

After a year off, Stephen applied to Calvary Bible College in Kansas City, Missouri, which was a gateway to his calling from God! Christ blessed Stephen at Calvary in so many ways. He developed friends that would see him through to the end of his life.

Stephen's walk with Christ and testimony was addictive. He had a smile that was sincere and genuine. Stephen was committed and dedicated to learning more about Christ. He had an abundance of faith. For his second year at Calvary, he packed up "Sheila," his car, and left for Calvary not knowing where his finances would come from. He had the faith in Christ to believe that He would meet his needs, and He did.

During his sophomore year, he had two part-time jobs. He was an ARA with the Dean's department at Calvary Bible College. He was also an after-school teacher at Meadowmere Elementary School through LINC, which stands for "Local Investment Commission." This was created to help and work with the community of Kansas City. The staff and students really loved Mr. Steve. Stephen and the site coordinator spent a lot of time talking about God and Heaven.

Stephen loved talking to his brothers in Christ at Calvary. They were a great source of strength and encouragement for one another. Stephen had a wonderful relationship with his brothers and sister. When the four of them would get together, they would stay up most of the night just talking and laughing. They supported one another as best as they could. The one thing I can truly say is that they loved each other so unselfishly. They would pray for one another, which was so rewarding to see for me as a parent.

Stephen held a very special place in my heart. I miss his smile, his late night calls, his hugs, and his kisses on my cheeks. He made sure he always told me that he loved me. The comfort and joy I have is in knowing that Stephen is complete in Heaven with Christ, and I will see him again. I thank the Lord that He allowed me to be his mom. He could have chosen any other mother, but He chose me.

ANTHONY REYNOLDS JR.

Stephen Phillip Reynolds. I remember my parents telling me that when he was born I asked if we could take him back. Ha ha! I was too young to understand at the time that we wouldn't just be brothers. He ended up being my best friend. Growing up was a struggle when Stephen had open heart surgery. My parents were so strong, trusting in God that he would heal Stephen and bring him through it.

We didn't always have a strong bond when we were young. Mostly because of me and my competitive ways, but he brought out the best in me when we played videogames. This little dude was hooking up games by the age of four or five. It was unbelievable! He turned into a very smart young man early on in his life as well. Everything seemed to come easy to him, math, science, etc. He always screamed and yelled for no reason. Ha ha! I thought he was nuts at first, but I ended up doing it too. We would laugh and joke about it all the time.

Playing jokes on each other was a normal thing in our household. You had to have tough skin if you got a joke played on you, and you better get back at whoever did it. When I moved out after my senior year in high school, on the morning our brother was taking me to McPherson, Kansas, I experienced something that changed the dynamic of us as brothers. Stephen started to cry because I was leaving. I didn't know what kind of impact I had on him over the years, and I started to tear up as well! Anybody in my family will tell you I don't cry very often. As the years went by, we got older, yet our relationship was the same. We always picked up where we left off.

Nothing ever changed. I remember the last time we talked he said, "I'm nervous, but I'm gonna ask Katie to marry me." So I responded, "Let me pray with you about it, man." At the end of our talk he said, "I love you, Bro," and I said the same in return.

When he passed away, it was hard for a few months. I struggled with it up and down for a while. I know without a doubt that God has given me all the strength in the world to get through it. He left such a strong impact on so many people before and after he attended Calvary. I noticed a big change on how he viewed life while going to school there. It changed our family as well. Stephen helped us become closer as a family than we ever were before. I'll be forever thankful to God for letting him live much longer than doctors said he would. God had plans for Stephen, and I know they were fulfilled! I love you, Bro. Rest well.

AUNDRA REYNOLDS

When I was asked to write something about my late brother, I won't lie, I avoided doing it. Part of me wants to say I don't really know why, but a more honest part of me reluctantly admits that maybe I just wasn't ready. Here I am, five years and some months after he passed away, and I'm just now putting my thoughts to paper. I have been avoiding it. Because I wasn't ready. Maybe I'm still not ready, but I think that I'll get there over time.

About Stephen, I have many thoughts, mostly pertaining to the kind of person he was and the kind of brother he'd been to me during my first nineteen years of life. No one really talks about it, but my birthday is closely associated with his homegoing date. April 27 is just three days before my own birthday, so I can't help but revisit thoughts concerning my brother and what his passing means to me each year as I celebrate my own birthday. Sometimes they're good thoughts. Other times I feel sadness, and I miss him, his laugh, his smile, and his presence. However, my mind inadvertently drifts to more uplifting thoughts whenever I feel myself sinking into a hole of depression, because you can't picture a smile like that or imagine a laugh so boisterous and not smile. It's impossible.

That's the kind of person Stephen was at his core. Sure, I can recant a plethora of stories about what being his little sister was like and the fights we got into and how he sort of nurtured me as an elder sibling, but they don't hold any value when compared to the stories I can tell about what being his sister in Christ was like. Stephen experienced not a drastic change but definitely a noticeable change when he began attending Calvary Bible College. During the few times he managed to make it home while attending there, I saw it. During the instances he returned to our home church, I saw it. Around his friends, the way they flocked to him like moths to a flame, I saw it. Around probably the only girlfriend in his life that I actually liked, I saw it. He went from a typical church-goer to a real man of God always on fire for the Lord. You could see it in the way people around him reacted to his presence, and that is how you know someone is truly different.

It was a gradual change but a lasting one. Stephen truly left a mark on the world, and the people he surrounded himself with can certainly testify how unforgettable he is. Truly a remarkable young man in every sense of the word. I feel I've been blessed with twice the future in Heaven of being his biological sister and heavenly sister as well. I look forward to seeing him once again. Soon and very soon. Because God is so good.

CHAPTER 21

Philippians 3:17, 20 - 4:1
Brothers, join in imitating me, and keep your eyes on those who walk according to the example you have in us. For many, of whom I have often told you and now tell you even with tears, walk as enemies of the cross of Christ. Their end is destruction, their god is their belly, and they glory in their shame, with minds set on earthly things. But our citizenship is in heaven, and from it we await a Savior, the Lord Jesus Christ, who will transform our lowly body to be like his glorious body, by the power that enables him even to subject all things to himself. Therefore, my brothers, whom I love and long for, my joy and crown, stand firm thus in the Lord, my beloved.

MEMORIES OF STEPHEN FROM HIS FRIENDS

This book would not be complete without hearing the stories of some of the young men who were friends with Stephen. All of these men met Stephen at Calvary Bible College. They were also some of the men who attended Stephen's funeral. They lived life together and laughed at ridiculously funny things. Stephen and his friends also grew spiritually together. Stephen's faith was inspirational because of his close, personal relationship with God. These are their stories. Some are funny, but all tell of the impact Stephen had on their lives as they grew together in their relationship with God as friends and brothers.

Levi Landrigan –

I first met Stephen Reynolds at the freshman orientation at Calvary Bible College in the fall of 2012. Steve's loud laugh and goofy personality made him widely known during the first few days. Steve and I first got to know each other when he came into my room that week, plopped down on my chair, and just asked "Levi, what's your testimony?" This caught me off guard because no one had asked me that question before getting to know me well! I told him my story, and he shared his. I was awestruck at his openness and honesty to someone he had only just met. I knew right away that there was something different about Steve. Shortly after that, an event transpired which would change every encounter the two of us had for the rest of the year. That event was a shortage of biscuits.

I walked into the lobby and saw my ARA, Troy, eating some of Mrs. Reynolds chocolate cake. Troy was sharing the cake with everyone, and I joined in to advertise her great cake. At one point, I had chocolate frosting all over my hands and said that the cake was "finger lick'n good." This instantly made everyone in the room hungry for some fried chicken. Steve and I hopped in the back of our friend Brandon's car and rode to Church's Chicken. We were concerned when we saw they were cleaning up inside and closing up for the day, but we were in luck! The drive-thru was open! We pulled up and placed a large order of chicken and 10 biscuits. There was a pause, and then we heard the woman on the other end of the drive-thru speaker say, "Ten biscuits? Ooooo! We ain't got ten biscuits!" We tried hard not to burst into laughter! I was trying hard not to laugh when Steve, pretending to be completely serious, glared at me and whispered harshly, "Levi, be quiet! They gonna to do something to our chicken!" As soon as the window rolled up, the car shook with laughter! Steve would ask me frequently to do my impersonation of, "Ten biscuits? Ooooo! We ain't got ten biscuits!" Even after everyone else on campus got tired of this event being retold, we would still share a good laugh about it.

As the school year went on, Steve and I grew closer and closer together as friends. My roommate had to leave Calvary in March. After that, I didn't like spending a lot of time in my room. I spent a lot of time with Steve and some of my other Calvary brothers in his room during the last month of Steve's life.

I am so glad God gave me that opportunity. During the many late nights we spent in Steve's room, I got to know him on a deeper level. We usually started just talking about our day. This would lead us to holding each other accountable in our faith and spending time in prayer. We would often spend time doing goofy impersonations, spinning freestyle raps, or discussing deep spiritual topics. I learned so much from listening and participating in these conversations. I grew a ton spiritually every night that I spent in Steve's room. After he went to be with Jesus, there was no one I wanted to be with more than the brothers who had been there during those late nights.

Steve had an incredible impact on my life, and he continues to inspire me to be a better man. Accountability, love, and fellowship were some of the things that Steve valued the most. I hold these things and the memories, as I press on in this life to glorify my King.

Stephen Buller –

I met Stephen Reynolds as a freshman when we both entered Calvary in the fall of 2011. I only knew Stephen from that August until his death, but I will always cherish and praise God for that time.

Steve was the best big brother I ever had. I grew up with one sister and no brothers, so when I came to Calvary and had a

CHAPTER 21

great band of brothers, I knew I had something special. Stephen and I had something called "Steve-Steve Time" or also "Steve-Steve Power!!" Since we were both named Stephen and spelled it the same way that was special. To describe this I will tell three different stories.

I remember the first time I saw Stephen. It was freshman orientation, and we got on the same van together. That's where the whole gang met for the first time, Jon, Justin, Ben, Kyle, etc. We were all there. Stephen was able to get us all going with introductions and teaching us the "grip, point, snap" handshake that he did with everyone. (Sorry you can't understand through writing what the handshake was.) But I remember that I was two rows in front of him on the van, and we leaned over to "shake" hands. Well, needless to say, I thought we would do a regular handshake, but Stephen wanted to do his "grip, point, snap." I totally did not know what to do, and as I failed to learn on the bus how to "grip, point, snap," all Steve did was look at me, laugh really hard, and say, "We will work on it later!!" We did, and I became a pro (not really). That is the first time I met Stephen Reynolds.

I remember two accounts that were big moments in our brothership. (I won't call it a friendship because it was more than that.) The first one is when we both really wanted to be dumb freshman and prank everyone in Stephen Hall. (That was literally the name of our dorm building. We owned the place, so we thought.) So we took my roll of Duct tape, and went to Troy Frasier's room. We Duct taped everything – his chair to the wall, his tooth brush to the door, his shorts to the ceiling, his shoes, and his pencils, etc. We thought we were so great and powerful. That Duct tape brought Stephen and I into a true friendship which escalated from there to brothership. Later that year in the spring, Steve was in my room with my roommate Ben. I walked in as Steve was on my iPod. He looked up at me and glared saying, "I see what you got on here!" I instantly thought I was in trouble. I thought he had found something weird or inappropriate (which was not on there). But after I look confused at him, he jumped up and yelled, "YOU GOT SOUL!! You listen to The Temptations, Kool and the Gang, Earth Wind & Fire???!!! WHY DIDN'T YOU TELL ME?????" We proceeded to dance and sing to the song "Treat Her Like a Lady" by The Temptations. Those songs, from then on, became big "study breaks" for Steve and me. We had something that a lot of people did not understand or want to understand. We had SOUL!!

Finally, the last story I wish to tell the readers is not like the other two. The first two stories show the funny, unpredictable, and fun character of Stephen Reynolds. If that's all he was, then he would have just been a friend, but he was a brother. This is why. One day, I was having a terrible time with a parent issue over one of the students in my youth ministry. I had just gotten a phone call that lasted an hour and had been one of the most draining experiences in my life, but I knew where to go. It was about 12:30 at night, and I knew I needed to find my best brother, Stephen Reynolds. He was in his room, extremely tired and on his bed. I walked in really slowly and plopped on his couch. All I said was, "Steve.....life is hard." He responded with a, "Ahuhhh........" Then we proceeded to have an inspiring conversation of grunts and huffs. I slept on his couch until 2:00 A.M. Though this was probably the most silent and seemingly meaningless conversation ever with Stephen, it is one that I will always cherish. Why? Because what happened in that room is that two men shared a heart of weariness and did not ever try to fix each other. Rather Steve and I sat in the pit of life's hardships and said with grunts and groans, "I understand, brother. I am right there with you." In that moment, there was no need for inspiring words or a big prayer time or a need to do anything. All that was needed was to sit there in the pit and say, "I know." This is an example I will always use for one of Steve's favorite passages, Ecclesiastes 4:9-12. In verses 10 and 11 it says, "For if either of them falls, the one will lift up his companion...Furthermore, if two lie down together they keep warm, but how can one be warm alone?" (NASB) Steve will always be my brother. His parents will always be Mama and Papa Reynolds, and I will always be looking forward to when I can have the next round of "Steve-Steve POWER!!!!!!!!!!!!!!!!!!!!!!!" Even better, when we meet again, Steve and I will have "Steve-Steve-Jesus Time." Oh, how sweet that day will be.

Troy Frasier –

I remember one day I was leaving the cafeteria. Four guys that I wasn't even sure I liked walked up to me and said, "Troy, you are an honorary member of the Wolfpack." "Yeah, join the Wolfpack!" Any one of you reading this is probably thinking, "Wolfpack? That sounds kinda immature and silly." Well, that was what I thought too. But one of those great guys I would get to know was Steve Reynolds, a man I liked at the time. I had no idea he would become my best friend and a true brother to myself and so many. But what was my response to this silly Wolfpack idea which sounded like an immature fraternity group? "Yeah, you can count me in, sure, sure." I had no intention of taking this seriously. But being new at the college, at the age of 20, in a new state, and trying to change my life completely for God, I had decided to be friendly to all and make as many friends as possible. I did not think of it again until a week later. I was up late in Steve's room which was not uncommon. In fact, about an hour every night of my college career for two years was spent in Steve's room. He looked at me and said, "This Wolfpack, it's a good idea. I think we could do big things." I asked him what he meant, and he started describing to me a simple idea of brothers really, truly holding each other accountable in our faith. At first I just kinda agreed that is sounded cool, but over time, I got to see it lived out. I got to truly see brotherhood and a family form from this idea. People from every walk of life, every background, and every group at school met together on this simple idea, "Let's hold each other accountable."

This then grew into something bigger, even though that group of people saw hard times, loss, and heartbreak of every kind. Our group of friends had to learn to confront blatant sin with people we met and covert sin with some of our closest friends. There were moments, so many moments, when we just came together, worshipped, and prayed together. It was not just Steve. Other great friends came and went, brothers in Christ I was privileged to know and love. Through it all, I got to walk with Steve, learn and grow together. We experienced legalism together and had to return to Christ from it.

It had all started late one night. On a night we should have been asleep or probably should have been doing homework, he looked at me and simply said, "We could do this. We could be onto a great idea." So many visions, lives, and moments were changed because it was decided the Wolfpack could be a spirit of worship and of living for God in all the fun we had. He and I learned to evangelize together, fast together, and court great women properly together. But of all that we learned, learning to create a real family, a real accountability group of brothers, probably is what I will remember. Forever. Psalm 133:1, "How beautiful it is when brothers dwell together in unity." (paraphrase)

Brenton Klassen –

Saturday, April 27, 2013, started out like any other lazy Saturday at Calvary Bible College. I woke up just in time for lunch and afterward headed to the library where I found Steve Reynolds working on homework. I sat down at the computer next to his. We both tried to work on homework even though we did far more talking and joking than studying or writing. We also kept an eye on the NBA finals, which were in full swing that weekend, by religiously checking NBA.com.

Around the middle of the afternoon, Kyle came into the library, and we began to preoccupy ourselves with a new idea that resulted in a cessation of all studiousness. We found an illegal live stream of an NBA game on a website and pulled it up on a library computer. Soon, through our creative genius, we were all listening to the game through a maze of splitters and headphones, while watching the live video stream. The Chicago Bulls and the Brooklyn Nets were playing a great game, and with our excitement, we were ruining any scholarly atmosphere that may have existed in the library.

It was during this happy ordeal that Jon Geiger came into the library and drastically changed our mood with a bit of news. He told us that he had just quit his job. Jon had been fed up with work for a while and had just decided to call it quits. He told us he felt uptight since he had quit without giving a two weeks' notice, and he no longer had a job. But he also felt relieved at the same time since he no longer had to worry about putting up with coworkers. Steve, Kyle, and I listened to Jon, and Steve gave him some fatherly counseling advice. Then we plugged in another splitter, and all four of us watched the game (which was a great game that went into multiple overtimes) until the librarian, Bridget Tomas, "kicked" us out of the library at 5:00pm because it was closing time. As we walked to dinner, we laughed about how we had gotten "kicked out" of the library.

At dinner, Steve got his usual bowl of Cocoa Puffs in chocolate milk. When he got up to get something, Jon put M&M's in his cereal. When Steve returned and started eating again, he didn't immediately notice, but he could tell that something was up by the smirks on our faces. When he tasted the M&M's, he was not happy, and he investigated by bellowing, "Who did this?" Somehow, Jon managed to blame Kelli H. (For a little while, Steve believed that Kelli had put the M&M's in his cereal, and he didn't complain. Soon, however, the truth came out. When Steve found out that Jon was the culprit, he reprimanded him for the prank. Jon felt bad and apologized.)

After dinner, Jon, Kyle, Mike Cousens, and I went to the gym to shoot hoops. I was on the gym list which enabled me to ask security to open the gym for us even though it was after hours. Since I was the only gym manager of the group that night, I was the responsible party for any emergencies that could happen while we were using the gym. As it turned out, an emergency did happen that night. We shot hoops for a while, and then we began to play two-on-two. Steve showed up during our first game of two-on-two in response to Kyle's text to come and join us. He was quite a sight in his Nike kicks, long socks, cargo shorts, Southpole beanie, and his favorite green hoodie. We were all glad to see him, and he shot on the other hoop to warm up while we finished up our competition.

The way we played was that whichever team reached 15 points first won. The losing team would then sub out one player for the person who was sitting, and we would play again. Mike and I won the first game, so Jon sat down. Steve and Kyle played against Mike and me. Steve was on his A game that particular night, and he and Kyle destroyed us. I was guarding Steve. I remember his pulling up and draining jump shots in my face, driving the ball to the hoop and laying it in over top of me, and doing many other things to help his team win.

When they won, their team should have stayed the same. Either Mike or I should have sat down, but Steve sat down instead. We knew that sometimes he needed a break because of his heart condition, and we asked him if he was okay. He nodded and told us to go ahead and play. While we played our next game, Steve left unnoticed to get a drink from the water fountain. We were too focused on our game, and we didn't pay any attention to the fact that he was gone until we were done.

When we finished, we started walking to the water fountain to get drinks. I was behind the other guys. I was just about to walk through the doors when Jon, who had gone through ahead of me, came sprinting out at full speed. "What's going on, Jon?" I asked. He didn't answer because he had already grabbed his phone and was dialing a number into it. I then walked through the door and saw what was going on. Steve was lying on the floor in front of the water fountain. "I'm calling security!" Jon yelled to us. "I'm calling 911," I announced. When I had gotten on the "approved list" to become a gym manager, I had been instructed that, in the case of any emergency, I should always call 911, even if I wasn't sure whether or not EMTs were needed. Even though I thought (and hoped) that Steve had only passed out and that he would soon come to, I immediately called 911. In the meantime, Mike and Kyle had gotten down next to Steve and were trying to communicate with him. A moment later, they dreadfully announced that he wasn't breathing and that they couldn't find a pulse on him. It was at this moment that we realized the gravity of the situation, and we began to pray.

Within a matter of seconds, David C. arrived. He had been holding the security phone. When he received Jon's call, he ran as fast as he could from the K-Bar to the gym. He was very professional in his assessment of the situation and immediately began chest compressions and CPR. Josh F. and other Calvary Security/Administrative Personnel also arrived quickly and took control of the situation in a professional manner. They cut off Steve's hoodie and connected him to a defibrillator which informed us, "Shock not advised. Continue chest compressions." During this time, I was on the phone with a 911 operator who was telling me to instruct those with Steve to do everything they were already doing.

Emergency vehicles began showing up eight minutes after I dialed. When they arrived, most of us were advised to leave the gym so that the professionals could have plenty of space to do their job. Kyle and I sat on the wooden platform outside the gym and prayed silently. It seemed like the emergency personnel were in the gym for an eternity, but finally they brought Steve out on a stretcher and put him in an ambulance. We then went back into the gym to get our things, prayed in there for a while longer, and then went to the chapel to join the rest of the student body in prayer.

I don't like to think about the rest of the evening. It consisted mostly of dark and dreadful anxiety in my spirit that morphed into a shocked state of disbelief when I heard the news that Steve had gone to be with the Lord. That night was the first night I didn't sleep a wink and was never even drowsy. I was awake all night talking, praying, and thinking. It was probably during this sleepless night that I began to fit together in my mind the ideas that I penned two days later during Monday's chapel. The sheet of notebook paper that I hastily pulled from my backpack that Monday morning during worship still had its blue-line ruling smudged by the tears that were falling from my eyes as I wrote the following words.

Steve was a gift of God to me. Steve was not only taken away; he was first given. I can't imagine what my life would be like if I had never met Stephen. He adopted me as his nephew and connected with me in a special way like only he was able to. Steve showed me how to find joy in the Lord. He showed me how to love God's people. He demonstrated a passion for the church and a living, joyful, and willing spirit that wanted to do work for the kingdom of God.

Josh Koops –

Well Katie asked some guys, including me, to write some memories about Steve for her book. I think a lot of the other guys will have memories to share about Steve, but I come from a different side. I only really got to know Steve a few weeks before his death. We did not hang out a lot and never had any one-on-one conversations. I remember laughing with him and the guys in the lounge at three o'clock in the morning, dancing in chapel to hymns, and playing Street Fighter on Xbox. However, Steve and I were not very close. It was at the end of my first semester at school that the Lord took Steve home, so I was unable to get to know him super well. But that is what was so amazing about Stephen Reynolds. I spent a grand total of maybe a week with him, and my life was impacted.

The conversations about school, girls, and divine election versus free will (we were at a Bible college after all) have not left me. Apart from that, the Lord has blessed me by giving me close relationships with many of the guys Steve was close to, and I have experienced Steve through them.

I also got to know Katie a lot during the summers of 2013 and 2014. I was around to witness her grieving and growing closer to the Lord through all the pain. I was around to help drive her to doctors' appointments, be with her and the guys at Steve's church, and watch how they all lived after Steve's passing. I've seen Steve's fingerprints on all of them and God's fingerprints on Steve through them.

Today the world is very focused on what we can grab for ourselves right now and how to get the maximum amount of fun for today, but Steve was focused on the future with Christ. He lives on in the memories of those in his godly legacy. Steve was not in this world very long, but we all remember him and remember the things God did through him. If the glory of God is man fully alive, then Steve glorified God. He was not perfect, and he was the first to admit it. He still struggled with sin every day, and he repented and sought a closer relationship with God every day. He was a leader of men, and he taught us how to lead other men as well. He loved God with all he had, and because of that, he loved us with all he had too.

"…faith, hope, and love. But the greatest of these is love." (I Corinthians 13:13 NIV) It really is true. What lasts is love, unconditional, Christ-like love. I don't know exactly what everyone else says Steve's legacy was. Others who knew him better would be better at describing him and how much of an impact he made. As a guy who barely knew Steve but has lived in close contact with those he was close to, I have seen the power of a life lived for the love of God and how it translated into love for others. Many people come and go from our school. We miss some and forget others. For some, we are thankful they're gone. How we live our lives today is important. Steve lived his life to love everybody – adult, child, peer, whomever. When they left Steve's presence, they had experienced a man who experienced God and lived in the joy of the Lord. That's my memory of Steve. No funny stories, no deep conversations, no crazy adventures – just a legacy that makes me look at myself deep down and wonder if I could live up to that. Just a legacy that makes me want to be better and makes me not want to be more like Stephen Reynolds but more like Christ. He did well. He finished well, and he set the bar high for us who follow. Thanks, Steve, I can't wait to meet up with you in glory and listen to all the rap songs you wrote with Jesus while waiting for us to catch up with you.

Mo Mitchell -

Stephen was more than a friend, and he was more than a brother. Stephen Reynolds was a role model. He set the example of what a man was to look like. It didn't matter who you were or what you were going through. Stephen could always put a smile on your face. I mean, that was just something he was able to do. Working with Stephen for a summer internship at City Union Mission was probably the coolest thing. We had the same routine all summer. We would wake up, workout, shower, get in the car, and, every single morning listen to the same song before work. My most vivid memory of Stephen was of him and me walking. He looked at me and said, "Bro, I look up to you." My mind was blown. I thought to myself, "This amazing man of God looks up to me." The one person I seriously looked up to as a role model had just said, "I look up to you." That is the one thing that will always stick with me. Stephen showed that he was a man of God each and every day. From the day I met Stephen to the day he was gone from this earth, he taught me how to be a man. He showed me how to be a brother. He showed me how to be a friend. Most of all, he taught me what it means to love like Christ.

Jon Gohdes -

Very few times do I remember "Reynolds" without immediately hearing his boisterous laughter ringing at the center of my memory. The man loved humor, whether it was about a funny dance, ten Church's Chicken biscuits, or a host of other things. As I reflect on this dear brother in Christ, it occurs to me that he was a very large man. I mean that in physical as well as spiritual ways. Allow me to explain.

For example, Stephen had very large hands. Whenever he would extend "the right hand of fellowship" to me, I would often notice just how huge his hands were, totally engulfing my seemingly puny ones. The significance rests not in the size of his hands but in what he chose to do with them. Stephen chose to serve his Lord and Savior Jesus Christ in a very "large" way. I observed and heard of him continually doing acts of kindness and compassion.

Also, Stephen normally had large bags under his eyes from staying up very late, sometimes just hanging out with friends and at other times encouraging and relentlessly interceding for his brothers before the throne of grace. It was not too uncommon for me to lie in my bed trying to fall asleep while my neighbor across the hallway, none other than Stephen Reynolds, loudly enjoyed the company of a host of friends who had taken up residence in his dorm room (often until 4:00 A.M.). Although God had not given me such grace to be able to do that, nor was I always thrilled that they were carrying on so, I deeply admired and respected my brother for his bold hospitality.

Additionally, Stephen had a large mouth but not one that spoke negativity or spread gossip—by no means! He was noticeably concerned with sharing the truth and encouraging fellow Christians. I would frequently hear him rapping profound statements of theology as well as many humorous or mundane things effortlessly rhyming without ever skipping a beat.

Stephen also had a large base of friends. He was a popular guy but not because he demanded friendship or strove to be liked by everyone else. Rather, he relentlessly reached out to others. He befriended jocks, nerds, and the outcasts who were among us. One confided in me some time later that Reynolds had a profound role in bringing spiritual restoration to him which otherwise would have not been encouraged.

It was no secret to anyone who spent five minutes with Stephen that he had a "large" laugh. He enjoyed life no matter the situation, but it wasn't because he refused to take life seriously. He took his calling and ministry very seriously. However, he could see a lighter side in every dark moment.

Finally, although many more commendable characteristics can be expounded, Stephen Reynolds had a large heart. This was true of him physically and spiritually. We discovered shortly after our friend passed from this life that his medical condition was due to an enlarged heart. His physical condition could not have been more ironically comparable to his spiritual condition because the man loved many people and loved them well. He loved his ailing fiancée, Katie. He loved his beautiful family. He loved his brothers in the Lord. Most of all (and most *evident* of all), he loved the Lord Jesus Christ who said that no greater commandments exist than to love God with all one's being and to love your neighbor as one's own self. Although he did not model these perfectly, Stephen's life was unmistakably marked by these two great commandments.

Daniel Frey –

Stephen Reynolds, when I say that name I think of a man. I think of huge smiles and constant laughter. Yet, in the same moment, there is calmness in the air. There is a peace that dismantles the walls that have become so commonplace in our lives. Memories of Stephen. While we shared little time on this earth, that is all it took to convince me that this man cared about people because he loved Jesus, and he wanted everyone to share with him in that joy. During one of the first conversations I had with Stephen, he asked me how I had met Jesus. This simple question has impacted me greatly. Since that time, every time I meet someone new, I am reminded to base my relationship with someone on Christ. Stephen desired to relate to people according to their relationship with Christ. If they did not know Christ, he wanted to share the hope of Christ with them. If they did know Christ, Stephen was excited to grow together in faith with his newfound brother or sister in Christ. Stephen saw the personal importance of one's relationship with Jesus and the powerful connection Jesus brings to human relationships. Stephen was an influential leader to all those around him. His humility, compassion, wisdom, and genuineness gave him the opportunity to speak into many people's lives. Since his death, I have spent many hours learning from the ways Stephen chose to live his life. He undoubtedly lived a life which demanded such observation.

CHAPTER 22

Psalm 30:11, 12
You have turned for me my mourning into dancing;
you have loosed my sackcloth
and clothed me with gladness,
that my glory may sing your praise and not be silent.
O Lord my God, I will give thanks to you forever!

MOVING FORWARD

It has been four years since I started writing this book. Life is very different now than it was during the sudden shock of losses at the beginning of this story. When I got sick it limited my life's mobility. There were so many things I could not physically do. When Stephen died, my dreams seemed to stop without the hope of a happy ending. Everything and everyone around me kept moving forward, yet I felt stuck in the middle of sickness and sorrow. Shock can do that to a person. Loss can do that to a person. I couldn't see the light in the midst of the storm. Now as I write to you, dear reader, six years since being poisoned by mold and five years from losing my intended fiancé, I can see the light more clearly. I find hope and joy looking back and seeing what God has done. There is also new hope and joy as I move forward in life.

My faith in God's goodness has strengthened my soul and

given me joy, hope, and endurance. To this day I would not change anything that has happened. I am stronger. My faith is deeper, and overall God's goodness has been seen by many people because of my story. You may disagree with me about believing in God. That's okay. Your broken spirit, dear reader, may someday find God as faithful, loving and good as I do today. Sometimes we have to become broken in order to see our need for a Savior. I grew up believing in God, but because of the trials I've experienced these past six years, I have more confidence in my faith after seeing what God has done through my hardships. No matter how difficult it has been, I would not change one thing. It was all worth it, and God's goodness shines on in my life!

Where is my health now?

My health has greatly improved. Each year since 2013 has held one or more major surgeries or medical tests. The surgeries have been hard on my body, but every year my body seems to get stronger. However, I am far from being well. Yet, despite my lack of health, I aim to enjoy life and live my life to the fullest in trying to honor God in all that I do.

I started using essential oils in 2016, and that has also greatly improved my health. I was a skeptic at first, but now I am a firm believer in the benefits of essential oils. A dear friend who also has had health problems since 2012 introduced me to DoTERRA essential oils. I firmly believe that these oils can and really do help a person's health. After all, God created plants to help us so shouldn't we use them when in need?

In July 2015, Mayo Clinic diagnosed me with chronic migraines, Fibromyalgia, and a weakened immune system. Mayo Clinic taught me how to moderate my life which has greatly helped my health. I have learned to listen to my body's different aches, pains, and fatigue. I know when I need to take a break and when I am able to keep going.

It has been hard for me to have a chronic illness when interacting with other people. Most people assume that you are sick only if you look sick. Even I can tend to think this way at times. However, that assumption is untrue. Chronic illness is often hidden and unseen by the human eye. Someone with a chronic illness, me included, may be very sick even though they don't look particularly sick. I have to remember I need to live in a way that is helpful and healthy for me whether people can understand it or not.

Am I working?

I have been able to work on a part-time basis since 2016. I work at an assisted living facility as a Medication Aide. I also serve as a cleaning lady for numerous businesses and private homes. I truly enjoy what I do. I get sick a lot during the winter time and have to cut my hours back. In the summer time, I am able to work more which is a blessing.

What does my social life look like?

After I had been sick for a few years, I began to think I wouldn't ever be able to do some of the fun things with friends I used to do. Hiking on trails, sitting around campfires, playing games, eating at restaurants, and so on seemed to be gone from my life. I wondered if I would ever be able to do those activities without feeling ill while doing them. At the beginning of my sickness, my friends still did activities with me, but it became normal for me to sit down or lie down and sleep out of sheer exhaustion.

Life looks so different now. As I've gradually regained some health and strength, I have been able to go on outings with friends without feeling so ill. I am able to take trips, visit, eat at restaurants, walk, minister to people, and kayak with different friends and family. In the past few years kayaking has become an enjoyable summer activity for me. Each year I have been able to do more in life and spend more time outside enjoying nature. I find great enjoyment in God's beautiful creation.

I have kept up with some of the friends I spoke of in this book. Carolyn, Jill Ann, Troy, and Buller will forever be my friends, and I enjoy picking up where we left off every time we get together. I have been enjoying making new friends and spending time with old friends since moving back to South Dakota in May 2015. I sometimes go on road trips to visit other friends. I have visited Kansas City multiple times since moving back to South Dakota.

I enjoy volunteering for different ministries at my church and other organizations. When I first got sick I started a letter ministry. I would write letters to the people God put on my heart to encourage and remind them they were not alone and that God is still good even in their trials. I have continued this ministry and enjoy encouraging people with my letters.

My friends would tell you that when I am with them I don't often act sick. I still smile and laugh and act quite normal. I have a very upbeat attitude in life. I'm an extrovert and it shows! I love being around people! I've learned to live in spite of my poor health, but I know when my body needs me to take a break or rest or even go home.

Do I still have a relationship with the Reynolds family?

I hardly knew the Reynolds family when Stephen died. However the summer of 2013 when the Reynolds invited me to their home and gave me my engagement ring began a lasting relationship with them. After Stephen died, I started attending church with the Reynolds. Mr. Reynolds is still the pastor there. They would invite me over on Sunday afternoons, and we would go out to eat. Mr. Reynolds, Mrs. Reynolds, Aundra, and I enjoyed spending lots of time together. Through that time and throughout the past few years, Aundra and I have become close. To this day I view her as a sister and friend.

I still keep in touch with them since moving back to South Dakota. Anytime I visit Kansas City I usually stay with the Reynolds. They love me like a daughter, and I love them like family. I was even invited to go on a family vacation with them one year. It was one of the best vacations I have ever experienced!

I don't know Chris and Anthony as well as I know Aundra, but they have been so supportive and encouraging to me since Stephen's funeral. We do not talk much, but we hope the best for each other. I see Stephen's two nieces and nephew every once in a while. Every time they see me I am welcomed with warm hugs.

I will forever view the Reynolds family as my family. I love them and care about them like I do my own family. They have brought me so many blessings and encouragement through the past several years. Being able to get to know the Reynolds family and experience life with them has just been more proof of God's goodness in my life.

Would I think of dating again?

Soon after Stephen's death, the idea of dating was not something I wanted to consider. Even the idea of moving forward in life was hard until I was able to work through the grieving process and shock. I have grown a lot and am able to go on dates again. That has been a huge step for me. In the past five years, I have been on a few dates but nothing ever fully clicked. Some people have asked if I was still holding onto the past. I have even wondered that myself. I have given this a lot of thought, and I really do not think I am still holding onto Stephen in that way. However, I also know that not every guy I go on a date with will be on the same page as I am.

Life has multiple journeys to experience. Dating after losing Stephen has been a new journey for me. If I ever fall in love again I hope to love that man, tackle life's good times and hard times together, and enjoy God with that man. God has grown me a lot in this area. I am very content with where God has me in this area of life. At this point, I am content in life as a single person. If God has a husband for me in the future, I will cherish and love that man until death. I won't regret being Stephen's intended fiancée, and I won't regret marrying my future husband if that is what God has for me. I believe God's plan is wonderful. I choose to enjoy my life and be thankful for all the blessings along the way.

Am I able to dream again?

The answer is, "Yes!" It has taken me quite a while, but I am able to dream again! I thank God for that. I have many dreams for my future. I lost my joy for a time as I processed through my losses, but today I have regained my dreams and joy for the future. I have seen God work in my heart to renew passions and dreams for things I had forgotten. I have seen new dreams appear, and I smile with excitement. Life is brighter these days.

Looking back, I see so many changes in my life. I see the many blessings that have come through the trials, and I know without a doubt that God was with me through it all. Looking forward I see many new possibilities, passions, and journeys ahead. I have gone through so much healing emotionally, physically, and spiritually. I would never have asked for this life specifically, but I wouldn't want to change any detail. I see God as my light and hope. Without my faith I wouldn't be who I am today. I found God to be good, and I have clung to His goodness and sovereignty. I feel more at peace about my hardships than ever before. I find excitement in sharing with people my story, a story of God's goodness.

A NOTE TO THE READER

Dear reader, yes, you! I don't know what you have gone through. The trials, tears, and losses you have experienced must be so hard. Because of the tears and pain in my life, I can relate on some level to the pain you are experiencing. If I could give you any encouragement it would be this, "DON'T GIVE UP!" Even if you feel like you are all alone, there is hope. Life doesn't always happen the way we want it to happen. Sometimes it can even seem hopeless. But remember this. Even in the hardest of circumstances we can find blessings. Cling to those blessings! They are there if you look for them. I hope, dear reader, that in those blessings you will find hope in Jesus. I hope that you will cling to the One who will never leave you. (Deuteronomy 31:6) Jesus is so worth it! Jesus will bring people into your life to help you carry your burdens. Sometimes those people simply appear as God brings them into your life at the exact time you need them. Other times you might have to go looking for them and ask for help. Either way, God knows what you need and is near you in your pain. There are people who want to help you. There is hope in the midst of our brokenness. God's plan is better than our own plans. Remember that! Also remember that God wants the very best for you, because He loves you. I hope and pray the very best for you too, dear reader. I hope you are able to find blessings amidst the pain. I pray that you find God and cling to Him. God is good, dear reader, even when life is hard. God is good!

RESOURCES

If you want to learn more about Christianity, I encourage you to talk with a pastor or a Christian that you know personally. Here are some other resources for you to dig into as well.

Websites:

www.gotquestions.org
www.biblegateway.com
www.proverbs31.org
www.answersingensis.org
www.icr.org (Institute for Creation Research)
www.summit.org
www.focusonthefamily.com
www.reviveourhearts.com

Books:

Bible
The English Standard Version (ESV), the New International Version (NIV), the New Living Translation (NLT), and are easier-to-understand translations of the Bible. I suggest starting by reading the New Testament section of the Bible. I specifically suggest reading the book of John first.

The Promise and the Blessing by Michael A. Harbin
The Case for Christ by Lee Strobel
Forensic Faith by J. Warner Wallace
Mere Christianity by C.S. Lewis
Why Suffering by Ravi Zacharias
Desiring God by John Piper

Podcasts:

The World and Everything in It (World News Group)
Todd White (Lifestyle Christianity)
Kyle Idleman
Proverbs 31 Ministries
Seeking Him by Nancy DeMoss Wolgemuth
Crazy Love by Francis Chan
Let My People Think by RZIM
Living on the Edge by Chip Ingram
Revive Our Hearts (Nancy DeMoss Wolgemuth)

Printed in the United States
By Bookmasters